WHAT MAKES A GOOD TEACHER?

This fascinating book explores the true essence of teaching, serving as a compass for both new and experienced primary educators. It explores the fundamental purpose and profound joy that comes with being a teacher, offering a perfect blend of research-based insights and practical wisdom, and the opportunity to reflect on your own values and your approaches to teaching.

Drawing on the authors' own experiences, each chapter weaves together evidence-based approaches with reflective practices, demonstrating how your authentic self – your values, beliefs and actions – form the foundations of effective teaching. Through engaging chapters on leadership, trust-building, resilience and the cultivation of kindness, this book offers clear pathways to:

- Develop inclusive classroom environments where curiosity and creativity flourish;
- Build a teaching philosophy grounded in children's rights and social justice;
- Navigate the challenges of modern education while prioritizing your wellbeing and mental health;
- Understand the unique qualities and skills you bring to the classroom.

Incorporating cutting-edge research, reflective questions and practical advice, this empowering guide provides the insights and inspiration you need to flourish as a teacher.

Whether you're a seasoned educator or just beginning your career, this compassionate and insightful resource provides the expertise and the challenges to make a lasting difference in the lives of your learners and helps you rediscover the satisfaction that comes from teaching at your best.

Karen McArdle is professor emeritus of education at the University of Aberdeen and an honorary professor at the University of Dundee, UK. She has spent a third of her working life in Australia and two-thirds in Scotland.

Alison Hurrell was a teacher of modern languages for 21 years in West Lothian, Scotland, before being seconded to reintroduce modern languages into the primary school. She then went into teacher education in Aberdeen, working with primary and secondary students and Continuing Professional Development in both sectors.

Penny Ogden has thoroughly enjoyed teaching in three very different English primary schools over a number of years. During this time, she always wanted to remain in the classroom. This included a wide variety of different management roles, which also included being part of the senior management and working as the lead practitioner.

John Forrester has over 23 years of experience working in both mainstream and special schools in England and Scotland. Between 2014 and 2020, he was the headteacher for a rural mainstream primary school and most recently the headteacher for a complex needs special school.

WHAT MAKES A GOOD TEACHER?

Values in Educational Practice

Karen McArdle, Alison Hurrell, Penny Ogden, and John Forrester

LONDON AND NEW YORK

Cover design: Jo Steer

First published 2026
by Routledge
4 Park Square, Milton Park, Abingdon, Oxon OX14 4RN

and by Routledge
605 Third Avenue, New York, NY 10158

Routledge is an imprint of the Taylor & Francis Group, an informa business

© 2026 Karen McArdle, Alison Hurrell, Penny Ogden and John Forrester

The right of Karen McArdle, Alison Hurrell, Penny Ogden and John Forrester to be identified as authors of this work has been asserted in accordance with sections 77 and 78 of the Copyright, Designs and Patents Act 1988.

All rights reserved. No part of this book may be reprinted or reproduced or utilised in any form or by any electronic, mechanical, or other means, now known or hereafter invented, including photocopying and recording, or in any information storage or retrieval system, without permission in writing from the publishers.

For Product Safety Concerns and Information please contact our EU representative GPSR@taylorandfrancis.com. Taylor & Francis Verlag GmbH, Kaufingerstraβe 24, 80331 München, Germany.

Trademark notice: Product or corporate names may be trademarks or registered trademarks, and are used only for identification and explanation without intent to infringe.

British Library Cataloguing-in-Publication Data
A catalogue record for this book is available from the British Library

ISBN: 978-1-032-67830-6 (hbk)
ISBN: 978-1-032-67760-6 (pbk)
ISBN: 978-1-032-67828-3 (ebk)

DOI: 10.4324/9781032678283

Typeset in Interstate
by SPi Technologies India Pvt Ltd (Straive)

CONTENTS

Introduction		vii
Grateful Acknowledgements		ix
What characteristics do children think make a good teacher?		x

PART ONE — 1

1. Society — 3
2. Values and teaching practice — 13
3. Why we do what we do, or vocation — 21

PART TWO — 31

4. Trust and resilience — 33
5. Kindness — 42
6. Courage — 50
7. Humility and empowerment — 58
8. Tolerance and patience — 65

PART THREE — 71

9. Things, place and time for children — 73
10. Wellbeing — 79
11. Nurturing — 88
12. Leadership — 97

13	Knowledge	106
14	Rights	116
15	Social justice: Gaps in society	124

PART FOUR — **131**

| 16 | Moving forward | 133 |
| 17 | Conclusion | 147 |

Index — 151

INTRODUCTION

Background to the book

At the time of writing this book, we four authors are troubled by politics and the instability in world affairs that affects everyone. In times of uncertainty, people seek to make policy and practice subject to safe and steady rules. There is a discourse in educational practice to do this. In our view education is highly complex and multi-layered and does not lend itself to easy measurable outputs. We prefer more qualitative outcomes to educational practice. This does not mean we choose not to measure in an educational context; rather we seek to colour bland and unidimensional performance statistics with an intelligent understanding of the way things are for teachers in the real world. This book is driven by our sympathy for and empathy with teachers, who mostly do the best they can in a context that is unstable and complex, yet they are subjected to measures of performance and expectations that are well-nigh impossible to meet. We hope this book will highlight some of these tensions that teachers deal with, and we hope we have provided approaches to resilience that will serve to encourage and affirm the value all four of us see in a teaching career.

The authors

We four have come together from very different backgrounds. We combine experience of selecting, educating, mentoring, leading and assessing teachers as well as bringing experience as primary school teachers, promoted teachers and headteacher. Two of us have worked in higher education for teachers in the past. We all have worked in England and Scotland mainly, but also in France, Australia and Germany. When four people come together, there are inevitably differences in what we think and choose to say. We have worked together to find consensus, and we do not expect you will always agree with us. We have written what we believe and what we have learnt from our experience.

Who the book is for

The book is written for a broad audience of teachers, student teachers and teacher educators in a primary school setting. Primary school teaching in the UK is characteristically for 5- to 11-year-old children. In the title we ask the question, 'What makes a good teacher?' Our answer is values, and values are of necessity subjective and are deeply held in our core. If your values are challenged and you find you are not convinced by us, we suggest you ask why and ask yourself what it is that makes you think differently, because values clarification has been a product of writing this book for us, and we urge you to follow a similar interesting and important process.

The book has been written following focus group discussion. We have included relevant literature and case studies of colleagues' or our own practice. At the end of each chapter is a summary of challenge questions, which you may wish to answer on your own or with students and colleagues. We also provide a summary of learning points. These are a part of our intention to assist with values clarification.

Outline of the book

The book is in four sections. Part One describes the background and context for the book and the implications for the good teacher. Part Two describes the qualities good teachers have and key priorities for which we strive, such as empowerment and wellbeing of the child. Part Three looks at environmental and conceptual ideas that will affect good teachers. Part Four considers how to move forward with the ideas from the book, and we draw our conclusions from the processes of writing this book.

Part One begins with Chapter 1 looking at society, the context in which we work and how that affects our practice. Chapter 2 considers values; what they are and why they matter because of the link to good teaching practice. Chapter 3 explores vocation, a rather old-fashioned term that we think needs to be revisited as it is about what motivated us to become educators in the first place and what keeps us going.

Part Two focuses on the virtues that we consider to be important for the good teacher. We consider virtues to be values in action. Chapter 4 is about trust, which we consider to be fundamental to the relationships we have with young children. Chapter 5 is about kindness. The theme of Chapter 6 is Courage which we consider to be important for all educators and this links to Chapter 7, which is about humility and empowerment and a discussion about where power lies and how this underpins relationships. This is not about having no fear, rather it is about overcoming fear. Chapter 8 considers tolerance and patience and the difference between these two qualities.

Part Three looks at some of the environmental and conceptual influences on teachers. Chapter 9 is about place, space and wellbeing of children. Wellbeing, which is the subject of Chapter 10, is often discussed but rarely defined, and we see it to be living a life of value for self and others. Nurturing is the subject of Chapter 11 from both a personal and school perspective. Chapter 12 is about Leadership which we consider is the role of people at all levels of the education and schools systems. In Chapter 13, we discuss where the knowledge comes from that we use in the classroom and wider school environment. Chapter 14 is about fundamental rights of the child, and we also consider a neglected subject of the rights of teachers. Chapter 15 discusses an aim we consider teachers should have, and this is social justice, which is closely linked to wellbeing for the child.

Part Three is about Moving Forward from the discussion of values. 'Moving forward' is Chapter 16, and this explains how the reader can learn and build on what has gone before in the book. Chapter 17 is our conclusion and our hope for the future of education. We focus in Part Three, in particular, on making a difference to children's lives both in and beyond the school.

GRATEFUL ACKNOWLEDGEMENTS

We thank all the teachers and pupils, whose experiences have motivated us to write this text. Their colourful lives have made our lives cheerful and colourful.

Thanks especially to Lynne Shiach, our critical friend, in commenting on the final draft.

Thanks to Charmian Wilby, who so expertly proofread the final text for us.

Thanks to Paul Ellie and Lily (not real names) for letting us include them.

WHAT CHARACTERISTICS DO *CHILDREN* THINK MAKE A GOOD TEACHER?

We would like to say thank you to: Amaya, Fatima, Iman, Hashir, Fajar, Mollie, Anna, Alia, Inaya, Azzan, Tayyiba, Ashaz, Saara and Alesha for their valuable opinions.

***

'Being helpful, being kind.'

***

'I think that the teachers should understand the abilities of us children, if they need help, if they need lots of help, or if they don't need help at all. I love teachers that genuinely want to help you, who listen to you too, who want you to thrive in and out of school. I also think that teachers should be strict, but only to a certain point so that the children understand what's good and what's wrong. Teachers should also be kind and loving and should have a good bond with the children. I love teachers that congratulate you for even the smallest things, even if other people thought that it doesn't matter.'

***

'A kind teacher who would explain something in a easy way and would be kind and caring.'

***

'I love having to move on every year, meet new teachers and let them become part of who I am. I love teachers that bring new things to learn every day. I have been here since the start of nursery, and I love the school itself, over the years I've had so many experiences that I'd never thought about doing before like climbing, horse riding, map reading, sailing and, my favourite, residentials. I loved coming to school everyday and learn new things, bond and be with my friends, and also make new friends. This school is a huge part of my life. I can't even imagine myself going off to high school. These teachers have made me ready!'

***

'When teachers are funny and make jokes. When they're kind and give you another chance.'

***

'A teacher who has a bit of a clown vibe. A teacher who is genuine and sometimes doesn't know stuff or something. A teacher who brings joy to others.'

***

'Understanding pupils – many children have different needs, support and a way of understanding education. I think a teacher should support, and help, children even if they are different from others and help them learn properly. Personally, I think teachers should be kind and respectful whilst teaching children and being optimistic about a child's future even if they struggle a lot. I think a teacher should love and have respect for themselves even when they have a bad day. Being patience and gentle when someone finds something difficult.'

***

'Being kind and careful with the children and loving. To be truthful and funny and like an aunty or uncle to a child. To be a trusted adult to children when something has happened to them.'

***

'Teachers are kind, and over the years I have realised that they take their time and money to do things for us.'

***

'When they are kind and when they make new people feel welcome.'

***

'When the children and teachers do a fun activity. It may cost money but it's all worth it in the end.'

***

'A teacher never gives up on you.'

***

'Just a teacher that is chill and like you can relate to and tell us about these stories and puts thing into their own stories and the children's perspective instead of being a robot or reading things straight out of a textbook. The teacher rewarding us for good behaviour. They make you feel safe, so you are not scared to express how you are feeling.'

***

'I think that a teacher should have a perfect type of explanation to explain all the subjects so that everyone understands and I think a teacher should also be kind so that the students don't stay stressed any time.'

***

'Being funny, kind and happy. A good teacher can understand what people are feeling.'

***

'(They should be) kind and trying to be helpful to children.'

***

'I see a person that is going to help me and my classmates achieve and learn new things, helping us reach hard goals we might have never thought about doing before.'

PART ONE

This section of the book describes features of the complex context in which we teach. It considers society and its impact on the values of teachers, parents and children. We explore motivation to teach, and we outline our understandings of values in educational practice.

1 Society

The social context

We all live in a particular society and culture, and this affects who we are, what our values and belief systems are and how these are lived out in our interactions with the children we teach. But first and foremost we need to acknowledge that the children we encounter, their parents' or carers' values, their community, their friends, the context of their lives, their home circumstances and their religious beliefs will not necessarily be aligned with our own, and this can lead to tensions unless we critically reflect on what our values are and from where they originated.

The social context for the child

Just as for the teacher, the society and culture we inhabit affects the development of the child. Bronfenbrenner (1977) proposed an ecological systems theory that views child development as a complex system of relationships, influenced by a series of interconnected environmental systems. He used the metaphor of Russian nesting dolls to describe the individual child embedded within multiple levels of context, time and practice.

Bronfenbrenner identified four systems that each contain rules, norms and roles that powerfully shape development. He called these the microsystem, the mesosystem, the exosystem and the macrosystem.

- **Microsystem**: This is the individual's immediate environment, which includes family, school and peer groups where face-to-face contacts take place. These relationships are highly influential and shape an individual's development. At this level, relationships have an impact in two directions, both away from the child and towards the child. The role of the teacher here is crucial in nurturing their development, scaffolding learning in a warm, caring and empathic environment.
- **Mesosystem**: This refers to the connections and interactions between two or more microsystems, like the relationship between a child's home environment and their school environment. So, for example, if a child is experiencing difficulties in school, it is likely

DOI: 10.4324/9781032678283-2

that the family will be forced to have more interactions with the school's teachers, and those family-school interactions will have an effect on the child.
- **Exosystem**: This involves settings that a person may not directly participate in but that still influence their development. Examples include a parent's workplace or a child's experience with community resources. A parent's job stress, for instance, can affect their interactions with their child and therefore impact the child's development.
- **Macrosystem**: This is the broadest level, encompassing the culture of the entire society and of racial, ethnic, regional or socioeconomic groups within a society. These societal norms shape the way individuals think, behave and interact with the world, and they endow individual life with meaning and value.

Bronfenbrenner later added the chronosystem – time. The chronosystem is the outermost level of Bronfenbrenner's ecological systems theory, focusing on the impact of the passage of time and how it affects both the individual and their environment. It also pertains to the historical context of the time the child is brought up in. For example, major historical events like wars or pandemics, technological discoveries or times of financial crisis can all impact the child's development.

Influences that affect children's learning

Cultural values, beliefs and practices change over time. Consider how ideas about when, if and for how long children should be educated, and how values and beliefs about early childhood education have evolved over the last century. Consider too the impact of technologies on the lives of the children and the teacher. A national survey of more than 15,000 schools, ordered by Rachel de Souza, the children's commissioner for England, found that 99.8% of primary schools and 90% of secondary schools have some form of smartphone ban (*Guardian*, 10 April 2025); language development was delayed by irregular contact with teachers and peers during the pandemic; and fine motor skills were underdeveloped as a result of 'swiping' hand-held devices. We suggest that inevitably there will be conflicting tensions with values, beliefs and practices changing over time and within contexts.

Tudge et al. (2017), expanding on Bronfenbrenner's understanding of the characteristics of the developing child, offer the following for our consideration and reflection.

> When a teacher ... has her first look at some children entering her class for the first time, what does she see? ... She sees girls and boys, some taller, some shorter, some fatter, some thinner. She sees children of different skin colors and one who has her head covered. Two children are speaking a language that she doesn't understand.
>
> (p. 48)

At the same time, the children will be looking at the teacher, picking up on a whole range of signs: Does the teacher look kind or strict? Will I understand what she says to me? How is she reacting to my hijab? Will she like me? What do I want and need from her?

This is how some of Penny's school children answered:

> **What would you like him or her to be like?**
> Just like a teacher, you can communicate with and one who doesn't shout.
>
> **When you meet a new teacher, what do you see?**
> I see a person that is going to help me and my classmates achieve and learn new things, helping us reach hard goals we might have never thought about doing before.
>
> **What would you like him or her to be like?**
> I would want them to have certain rules and they have to be strict when they need to, not shouting or telling everyone off all the time. I would also want them to be kind and understand everyones learning abilities.

Figure 1.1 Comments from Penny's pupils

Figure 1.1 shows comments from Penny's pupils. As teachers, we know that only by observing the children as they engage in the activities we have devised, by listening closely to their conversations with their peers and by interacting with them will we be able to learn about their experiences, the values and beliefs they bring from home and their current levels of competence. And the teacher's belief in the ability of all children to learn, with support and scaffolding, as Vygotsky (1978) posited, can only enhance children's experience of schooling.

Influences, therefore, can be global, country-wide, regional and local. Global influences include climate change and immigration, for example. Climate change affects the curriculum, in particular, as we aim to educate for an uncertain climate future and changing fauna and flora in the environment. Immigration affects us in many ways. For example, Penny taught a group of 18 children in England from within a large, transient year group. This diverse group came from 12 different countries, speaking 11 different languages. The school's pupil population has 44 different languages. Apart from the learning challenges, a significant number of children had attended at least two or three schools by the time they were 10 years old, with one child having been to five schools!

Global migration is a significant factor affecting children; some children move, having experienced sudden upheavals from their home country, due to discrimination or government policy. These factors can have a huge impact on a child's readiness to learn, despite their willingness and ability; therefore teachers are required to use a wide variety of skills, in addition to using considerable empathy and understanding – core values we would suggest. Pupils may also be transient, moving from one place to another for residence. This increase in English as an additional language (EAL) pupils places new and additional demands on the primary school educator.

Country-wide influences include political decisions, which affect learning and teaching. By the very nature of government timescales in the UK, Australia, the USA and many other countries, educational policies may be time-limited according to the term of office of a government. This means short-term policy may be preferred over longer educational interventions. The impact on the teacher can be a never-ending stream of new initiatives to be built into an already packed curriculum, leading frequently to undue stress and burnout. The state of the economy and interpretation by politicians of solutions to downturns will affect the money made available to schools generally. The increase in poverty currently being experienced in the UK because of the so-called cost of living crisis affects schools in many ways. Children may arrive hungry to school or poorly dressed and tired. This affects learning and accordingly the role and practice of the teacher. Interventions such as providing breakfast and clothing swaps, as well as carefully paced learning opportunities, have increasingly become part of the role of the teacher in the UK.

Regional factors that influence the teacher may be the degree of ruralness or urbanness of the school. Rural schools in the UK may need to work with small numbers of pupils, for example, and with pupils travelling long journeys to school. Local issues can also influence learning and teaching, not least the opinions of parents and carers. They can be avid supporters of schools or a source of criticism that is local and direct. In the following section, Alison describes a rural primary school.

Alison explains ruralness, Vygotsky and the 'more knowing' other

Isobel is the teaching head of a small rural primary school in Moray, Scotland. There is one other member of staff, and there are two classes in the whole school: P1-P3 (ages 5-8) and P4-P7 (9-11). Isobel teaches the older pupils. Because of the composite nature of the classes, it is not possible to engage in a linear learning and teaching programme of the formal curriculum, and the teachers have been experimenting with thematic approaches, which allow the children to engage at their current level of competence with more experienced others. For example, some P2 children (in the composite class) are more competent and confident readers than those in P3. Some P1 children respond better to the delights of number work than their older classmates.

You will probably have heard in your teacher education programme that Lev Vygotsky introduced the concept of the zone of proximal development (ZPD), which he defined as:

> the distance between the actual development level as determined by independent problem solving and the level of potential development as determined through problem solving under adult guidance or in collaboration with a more capable peer.
>
> (1978, p. 86)

Read on! Sometimes a novel will be the focus of the children's learning and teaching, and the teacher weaves different aspects of literacy, for example, through the characters, the setting and the plot, with each member of the class contributing according to their skills and their interests. Vygotsky's ZPD can be seen in action, and it is heady, convincing stuff! Children may engage in art and design to illustrate the landscape, the timelines of the novel or the physical traits of the characters, as they imagine them to be. They explore relationships, conflict resolution and health and safety issues as they might arise in the novel. Mathematics are skilfully taught when considering quantities for favourite recipes, for distances, or for the passing of time.

Differentiation on the part of the teacher is by task, by interest, by the amount of support needed and provided, by the length of time given to the task and by the end-product. The creative opportunities abound. The formal curriculum is thus embedded, and by the very nature of the composition of the classes, the informal curriculum is equally embedded. The children are respectful of, and benefit from, their 'more knowing' classmates (as one of Isobel's composite class pupils said), no matter how old they are. The learning takes place in a familial atmosphere. Such are the challenges of small rural schools. But oh, it is a privilege to see it in action!

Social influences, such as the small rural school, can be challenging, but as teachers we hopefully know we are both making a difference and are highly relevant to the social context in which children live. Another positive way of thinking about teaching and society is to think about culture. Culture may be defined in many ways, but here we are using it to mean the 'values, customs, beliefs and symbolic practices, by which men and women live' (Eagleton, 2016, p. 1). Through creating the culture of the community in the school and showing cultural sensitivity, we are reflecting and enhancing the identity of the society in which the school is located. We can model good values from society, and we can share perspectives and engender mutual understanding through, for example, participating in events such as World Languages Day or Faith Week in the UK.

Values in the social context

The social context for teaching is complex but very rich. Perhaps the most important way of responding resiliently to teaching pressures is to hold tightly onto our sense of vocation and onto our core teaching values. This means we are treating children in a way that is carefully thought through and is sound. Values may be understood as deeply held beliefs that direct our behaviour. They embrace broad preferences concerning courses of action or desired outcomes. A code of ethics or values is based on an assumption about universal human rights. What makes them universal is the profound mutuality of experience that characterises human life (Ransome, 2013). Our values contribute to the kind of teacher we are or want to be. We propose that knowledge of who we want to be as a teacher leads to confidence and autonomy.

There are many examples from history of values being held that define the protection of human rights. The 1948 Universal Declaration of Human Rights of the United Nations General Assembly asserts 'the inherent dignity and inalienable right of all members of the human family.' Our own core values are drawn from a strong collective notion of what is right and our own strong individual ideas (McArdle, 2018).

We need to discuss whose values we commit to, as well as our own. Values of equality, inclusion and diversity are frequently mentioned in relation to teaching but have become a little tired over time, and it is not always clear what they actually mean in practice. The General Teaching Council, Scotland (GTCS) provides a set of different values with a detailed explanation of what they mean, which we find helpful. Here we present the descriptions of social justice, trust and respect, and integrity.

8 *What Makes a Good Teacher?*

The GTCS Standard also gives more practical guidance on what this means in practice. The following selected examples are given *inter alia* for social justice practice:

> **Social justice**
>
> Social justice is the view that everyone deserves equal economic, political and social rights and opportunities now and in the future.
>
> **Trust and respect**
>
> Trust and respect are expectations of positive actions that support authentic relationship building and show care for the needs and feelings of the people involved and respect for our natural world and its limited resources.
>
> **Integrity**
>
> Integrity is the practice of being honest and showing a consistent and uncompromising adherence to strong moral and ethical principles and values.
>
> GTCS Professional Standards, 2021

- Building and fostering positive relationships in the learning community which are respectful of individuals.
- Embracing global educational and social values of sustainability, equality, equity, and justice and recognising children's rights.
- Respecting the rights of all learners as outlined in the United Nations Convention on the Rights of the Child (UNCRC) and their entitlement to be included in decisions regarding their learning experiences and have all aspects of their wellbeing developed and supported.
- Demonstrating a commitment to engaging learners in real world issues to enhance learning experiences and outcomes, and to encourage learning our way to a better future.
- Committing to social justice through fair, transparent, inclusive, and sustainable policies and practices in relation to protected characteristics, (age, disability, gender reassignment, marriage and civil partnership, pregnancy and maternity, race, religion and belief, sex, sexual orientation) and intersectionality.
- Valuing, as well as respecting, social, ecological, cultural, religious, and racial diversity and promoting the principles and practices of sustainable development and local and global citizenship for all learners.
- Demonstrating a commitment to motivating, and including all learners, understanding the influence of gender, social, cultural, racial, ethnic differences and that everyone deserves equal economic, political and social rights and opportunities now and in the future.

(derived from GTCS Professional Standards, 2021)

Helpful though these are, we also need to be aware of our own values and beliefs and synthesise these with the professional standards. There are many interpretations of social justice, and we present some of them here. For example, recent egalitarian writing has become dominated by the view that the fundamental aim of equality or social justice is to compensate people for undeserved bad luck. This includes things such as *being born with poor native endowments, bad parents, and disagreeable personalities, suffering from accidents and illness, and so forth* (Anderson, 2004, p. 155).

Rawls (2001) describes social justice as fairness, linked to reciprocity and collaboration amongst people to realise fairness. Dorling (2015) describes five reasons why social inequality or lack of fairness persists:

1. **Elitism is efficient**: Dorling describes how some people try to defend the notion that elitism is natural and that some people are labelled as being of 'limited ability' and so cannot be equal.
2. **Exclusion is necessary**: This tenet argues that exclusion is unavoidable as a natural phenomenon. Good luck and bad luck are unavoidable.
3. **Prejudice is natural**: Dorling explains how lack of respect for people above or below you is widespread.
4. **Greed is good**: The rise of elitism, exclusion and prejudice were all precursors of the age of greed in the 1980s in the UK and have led to wide-ranging inequalities.
5. **Despair is inevitable**: Growing despair is the result for those living in the most elitist affluent societies, where inequalities are allowed and indeed encouraged.

Dorling (2015) discusses how this affects children.

> In response to growing inequalities and unsustainability, the consequent curving upwards of rates of depression and anxiety is closely connected to how children are treated, how they are ranked, and how they expect to be treated later, when they are adults.
>
> (p. 11)

A capabilities approach to injustice is perhaps relevant to teachers. One's capabilities can contribute to social justice; they are not a function of fixed personal traits or character, but of changeable traits, social relations and community norms (Anderson, 2004). Accordingly, for the teacher, this means that capabilities that contribute to social justice can be taught. We suggest that this means assisting all children to know they are equal; this is to be done in the knowledge that they are in fact living in a rather unequal society.

The challenge questions at the end of this chapter are intended to help you to clarify your thoughts about one value that may be resonant with you: the value of belief in social justice, which is a prescribed value in Scotland. You may not believe in social justice, but we hope you do. Values emerge in our behaviour, sometimes unwittingly, so it is helpful to know our own values. Critical reflection and reflexivity are central to discovering our own values and beliefs in practice.

Critical reflection

Teaching as a discipline is socially constructed and is different in different countries. Shafer-Landau (2012) in an anthology of ethical theory suggests that there are two questions at the heart of thinking about ethics and values:

- What should I do?
- What kind of person should I be?

The social construction of teaching implies that there are boundaries and *doxa* (rules or habits) that may limit us and our freedom to do what we want to do for the child. We may well participate though a social unconsciousness in the system of socially constructed learning and teaching. Being critically reflective is crucial to knowing what we value as individuals and to justify the ethical choices we make about children and learning and teaching. Wallace and Poulson (2003, p. 6) define being critical as follows

Being critical

- Adopting an attitude of scepticism or reasoned doubt;
- Habitually questioning the quality of claims to knowledge;
- Scrutinizing claims to see how far they are convincing;
- Respecting others as people at all times;
- Being open-minded;
- Being constructive.

This description of criticality is useful as it is implicitly full of virtues of respect, broad-mindedness and a constructive attitude to others (McArdle, 2018). We discuss reflection and values as important to critical reflection. Reflexivity is different from reflection but is related; it is about challenging our own assumptions. Bolton (2014) provides the following definition.

Reflexivity

> To be reflexive is to examine, for example the limit of our knowledge, how our own behaviour plays into organisational structures, counter to our own personal and professional values, and why such practices might marginalise groups or exclude individuals. It is questioning how congruent our actions are with our espoused values and theories (e.g. about religion or gender).
>
> (p. 7)

This quotation sets out examples of how one can be reflexive. It helps us to understand reflexivity if we think of something that goes back on itself like a reflex angle in geometry. Internal dialogue and support of trusted others can help us with this meta-thinking.

A creative tension may exist between our espoused values and our practice. To put it simply, everyone we know in education is likely to say they believe in equality, but their understandings of its meaning and of equality practice may be quite different (McArdle, 2018). We may not always act according to our value base. Discomfort with our own practice is a useful means of being reflexive and discovering when this creative tension is happening.

Educational sociological questions usually reflect values. One definition of education is provided by Meighan and Siraj-Blatchford (1998, p. 14):

> A structural functionalist view of education tends to stress the activity of schools in training and selecting children, so they fit into some necessary slot in a relatively harmonious society.

This may seem rather harmless or bland as an explanation of education. Meighan and Siraj-Blatchford qualify this statement.

This view implies that children need to be manipulated in some way for that society's convenience or for some other reason. The images used by people who take this view stress this. The teacher is said to be like a potter moulding clay or like a gardener cultivating plants, or a builder building a house on sound foundations. In each case pupils are seen as things to be possessed and often have no rights.

(1998, p. 14, cited in McArdle, 2018)

These two quotations show how complex values are in the sociology of education. In this chapter we have explored the influence of society on education and teachers, and how this is linked to the values we hold as individuals in both our personal and professional life. We hope we have motivated you to be challenging and critical of yourself and your values and to explore how they influence your behaviour in teaching and learning contexts. The following challenge questions are intended to help continue this reflective and reflexive process.

Learning points

1. We all live in a particular society and culture; this affects what and who we are, teachers and children alike.
2. Values: Our values contribute to the kind of teacher we are or want to be, and how we interact with the children in our classes.
3. Human rights/GTCS standards are important as examples of professional standards, but we also need to be aware of our own values and beliefs and synthesise these with the professional standards.
4. Social justice is about fairness, and fairness in school is very important.
5. Critical reflection and reflexivity are important ways in which we learn about our values and our assumptions about education.

Challenge questions

1. What is the most important thing about you as a teacher?
2. What for you is non-negotiable about teaching?
3. What is the best thing you do as a teacher?
4. What do you think you need to work on as a teacher?

For questions 5-7, list all the things that you or others do as a teacher.

5. Which things are directly linked to learning and teaching?
6. Which things are to do with pastoral care?
7. Are there any things there that you think should NOT be on the list?
8. How does your school, and how do you, tackle big social issues like democracy and climate change?
9. What do you think makes some people more equal than others in society?
10. What is the role of the teacher in social justice?
11. What can you do as a teacher to help overcome social injustice?

References

Anderson, E. (2004). Against luck egalitarianism: What is the point of equality? In M. Clayton & A. Williams (Eds.), *Social justice*. Blackwell Publishing, Malden, MA.

Bolton, G. (2014). *Reflective practice: Writing and professional development* (4th ed.) Sage, London.

Bronfenbrenner, U. (1977). *The ecology of human development: Experiments by nature and design.* Harvard University Press, Cambridge, MA.

Dorling, D. (2015). *Injustice: Why social inequality still persists*. Policy Press, Bristol, UK.

Eagleton, T. (2016). *Culture*. Yale University Press, New Haven, CT.

General Teaching Council for Scotland (GTCS). (2021). Professional Standards 2021.

McArdle, K. (2018). *Freedom research: Becoming an autonomous researcher*. Palgrave Macmillan, Cham, Switzerland.

Meighan, R. & Siraj-Blatchford, I. (1998). *A sociology of educating*. Cassell, London, UK.

Ransome, P. (2013). *Ethics and values in social research*. Palgrave Macmillan, Hampshire, UK.

Rawls, J. (2001). *Justice as fairness: A restatement*. Harvard University Press, USA.

Shafer-Landau, R. ed. (2012). *Ethical theory: An anthology*. John Wiley & Sons, Oxford, UK.

Tudge, J.R.H., Merçon-Vargas, E.A., & Payir, A. (2017). The importance of Urie Bronfenbrenner's bio-ecological theory for early childhood educators and early childhood education. In L. Cohen and S. Stupiansky (Eds.), *Theories of early childhood education: Developmental, behaviorist, and critical* (pp. 45-57). Routledge, New York.

Wallace, M., & Poulson, L. (2003). *Learning to read critically in educational leadership and management.* Sage Publications, London.

Vygotsky, L.S. (1978). *Mind in society: The development of higher psychological processes*. Harvard University Press, Cambridge, MA.

2 Values and teaching practice

Introduction

One of Karen's favourite teachers was a secondary school teacher called Mrs. Stuffins. She was small and round and very, very kind to all the pupils. She never raised her voice, and she laughed all the time. She valued every child individually; she had no favourites and valued us as a class too. She also valued the school as a community, in which she did her best to teach us English language and literature using modern, exciting texts as well as the more worthy curriculum texts.

Thinking back to that time when Karen and her classmates were troublesome 14-year-olds, it was clear Mrs. Stuffins valued all the pupils equally and positively without exception as potential learners.

Karen also remembers an elderly, skinny primary school teacher called Mrs. Beese, who did not like Karen, and Karen does not know why. We, as a class, were learning our times tables, and when we got to the ten times tables and could repeat them all by rote, we got a prize of a sweetie. When Karen completed this task, Mrs. Beese said she had stopped giving sweets as Karen was so far behind and had taken so long. This was simply unfair as half the class had yet to reach this point. Karen said she felt sick, as she knew the teacher did not like her, and she was overcome by the lack of fairness. Mrs. Beese said, 'don't be so stupid,' and Karen vomited on the floor. Mrs. Beese sent Karen downstairs to the sick room, which was good as Karen felt very sick at being so disliked.

Thinking back, it is a surprise that Karen remembers this small incident from so long ago. Teachers probably cannot like all children, but treating them equally is important. Children are very sensitive to unfairness. Mrs. Beese did not value Karen and did not think it necessary to pretend she did.

Penny remembers one of her teachers:

> Nuns can often get a bad press from previous generations, but my favourite teacher was a wonderful nun, who always listened, was always kind and from my young perspective always smiled! She was also excellent at encouraging you whether it was with Sports, or Maths, Music, or Art.

Values

The subtitle of this book is 'Values in Educational Practice.' The preceding anecdotes show how values make such a difference to children's experiences. We and you, as educators, use values talk all the time. We use expressions like 'good' or 'bad,' 'better,' 'the best' (Orsi, 2015). The term 'values' itself is used in lots of different ways. In this book, we think values are deeply held beliefs that affect how we behave in an educational context. Values have become a little tired, we suggest, and there is the danger that espoused values become a sort of checklist. Equality, inclusion, diversity and other similar behaviours or outcomes that we should arguably aspire to are in danger of becoming things that we just tick off from the curriculum. To us, the authors, these values need to be kept alive as they are central to a positive experience of school for all children. In this book, we are also thinking more broadly of moral beliefs and ethical standpoints. The words 'morality,' 'values' and 'ethics' overlap, and we use the term 'values' to communicate this combination. We are not moral philosophers and so do not seek to define too closely these terms, which are themselves contested.

The main title of this book is *What Makes a Good Teacher?* and we intend to explain that values in action, known in an old-fashioned sense as virtues, are important. When thinking about education, we often think about outcomes linked to knowledge, skills and attributes. All of these are important and are discussed in the book. Knowledge and skills for teachers have been written about a lot but attributes or qualities for teachers less so. We see virtues as being attributes or values in action.

We do not intend to assert specific values that should be applied in education; rather we want you to be thinking about your own approaches to, and choices for, education. This book seeks to make explicit the ways in which our own values underpin and influence our approaches and choices.

- If a teacher believes all children should reach the same endpoint, she or he will work more with some children than others;
- If a teacher believes all children should be treated exactly equally, she or he will work with the whole class in the same way.

We wish to remind the reader that thinking about what is right and wrong involves making judgements, and we have inevitably set implicit standards of what right and wrong actually mean for us the authors (McArdle, 2018). Values can be defined as broad preferences concerning appropriate courses of action or outcomes. Values have the interesting capacity for both expressing underlying belief and providing motivation to act in particular ways (Ransome, 2013).

Values therefore represent a person's sense of right and wrong in the context of what ought to be and are broad preferences for appropriate courses of actions and outcomes. Increasingly values are seen as being culturally relative. Karen found this out when reading about resilience, which is discussed in Chapter 4; it is sometimes thought to be about bouncing back if one is knocked over. Some Southeast Asian countries think of resilience as not being knocked down in the first place. We only have to think about how some countries teach largely by rote to see that there are different ways in which different kinds of education are valued.

Exactly who decides what is right and wrong for education is multifaceted. Education is socially constructed; it has a history and has not always been the same, but history often lingers. We wish here to say that governments, policy makers and education authorities are not always the quickest at making change happen or reflecting change in society.

Favouring something or deciding it is a value for you can be thought of in three ways (derived from Orsi, 2015, p. 118):

1. **What kind of attitude it is**: A desire, a practical stance or belief, an emotion or a combination of these;
2. **Its direction or cause**: For whom or for what;
3. **Its intensity**: How much stronger than your attitude to other beliefs.

If something is non-negotiable for you, it is almost definitely a value. For example, for Karen McArdle racism is non-negotiable, and accordingly equality is a value for her.

Where the book comes from

Alison Hurrell and Karen McArdle, two of the authors of this book, undertook a piece of qualitative research together to explore what made teachers good at what they do. We interviewed so-called good teachers and found that the reputed goodness was different for different teachers (McArdle, Hurrell and Munoz Martinez, 2013) and was linked to values and virtues. We identified a confluence, or flowing together, of philosophy, pedagogy, classroom practice and underpinning values. Teachers were consistent and congruent within themselves with a balance of philosophy, pedagogy, values and classroom practice, all directed towards the wellbeing of the child. The good teacher, we found, was a teacher with strong child-centred values.

We found ourselves focusing on values and virtues, defining virtues as values in action, as mentioned before. It became apparent to us the confluence, as described earlier, as well as virtues was important—not a checklist of virtues that could be learnt but a balance of virtues in the personality of the teacher. The traits or virtues presented in this book are not a checklist but a description of those qualities that matter. In short, teachers are not *good* because they can tick off virtues; they are *good* because of who they are.

Expertise is, as Carr (2003) suggests, a matter of constant creative interplay with the needs and challenges of the pedagogical occasion, and Van Manen (2007) further suggests that 'the act of practice depends on the sense and sensuality of the body, personal presence, relational perspective, tact for knowing what to say and do in contingent situations' (p. 20).

One of our research participants was Eva. She describes what she thinks makes a good teacher.

> Yes. Having a presence in school ... but I think listening to children, listening to find out about them, find out who they are, to remember that children are all individuals. The thirty-three children in my class are thirty-three different children ... I would like to think I know a lot about every single child.
>
> (McArdle et al., 2013, p. 87)

16 What Makes a Good Teacher?

Kevin, a headteacher, is quite different in his response to the same sort of question.

> Right, well I think … a bit of realistic expectation of the children and their families. We have pressure from above in terms of raising attainment and closing the gap but, as teachers, we need to be realistic about that and take it a step at a time. I think we need empathy.
>
> (McArdle et al., 2013, p. 88)

This research showed us how different individuals were different in their knowledge, skills and qualities but were all good in their different ways, which led us to consider the qualities in more detail and to write this book with its emphasis on virtues or values in action.

Pring (2004) distinguishes between moral virtues and intellectual virtues. Moral virtues include courage, perseverance, honesty, caring for others, welfare and concern for others. Intellectual virtues refer to truthfulness, openness of mind, concern for accuracy, interest in clarity of communication and impartiality.

> By virtue, I mean the disposition, deep and enduring which motivates a person to pursue a course of action, despite difficulties and challenge, which the person conceived to be good and appropriate. Any list of virtues, therefore, embodies the values which prevail in a social or cultural tradition.
>
> (Pring, 2004, p. 184)

In this quotation Pring refers to the social and cultural traditions and how these affect the way we think about values. In order to be aware of these influences on our own values we need to be reflexive (see Chapters 1 and 3), which means challenging taken-for-granted assumptions.

Thinking with morality: What I ought to do

Rachels (2007) discusses morality and describes a common-sense view that morality or ethics demands that we balance our own interests against the interest of others. Of course, we look after our own needs, but at the same time, the needs of others are also important. Egotism or narcissism is the opposite of this, where people only look after themselves. Morality is complex and not like a science, where circumscribed answers are put forward, nor is it simply just likes or tastes. (Malik, 2015). It requires us to think deeply about it.

Dworkin (2007) discusses judgements we make.

> We evaluate not only what we should do now, but what we have done in the past. We judge not only actions but persons, policies, character traits, desires, thoughts, institutions. We judge not only whether actions are right but whether they are courageous, virtuous, cruel, excusable, sentimental, above and beyond the call of duty, sincere, just, and so forth.
>
> (p. 785)

Thinking about how we develop our beliefs, Dworkin (2007) describes the following ways:

- From religious teachings;
- Golden rule considerations (How would you like it if Johnny wouldn't let you play with his toy?)

- Appeals to consistent behaviour (You remember not wanting to play with Harry because you thought he was mean. Aren't you behaving the same way?);
- Appeal to procedure (What would be a fair way to pick teams for the game?)
- Weighing up competing ideas (What do you think is more important? Telling Sue she looks pretty or being honest and saying her new haircut does not suit her?)
- Appeals to parts of the decision-making process (Perhaps you ought to wait before deciding, so that you are not so upset);
- Appeals to virtues (You lie because telling the truth would make you unpopular);
- Appeals to moral authority (If you are having trouble deciding what to do, how about you ask your parents or a teacher?).

(Derived from Dworkin, 2007, p. 788)

The purposes of education

Exactly what education is or should be is rightly contested, and the authors' ideas underpin all of this book. Here we draw on the idea of Thomas Pring (2015), and we return to this theme in Chapter 10: Wellbeing.

> Education nurtures the distinctively human qualities and capacities.
>
> (Pring, 2015, p. 28)

This quotation is qualified by Pring with the question, 'But what are the qualities and capacities associated with being a person?' (p. 28).

The purposes of education, suggests Pring, may be associated with human flourishing. Pring quotes White (2003) describing flourishing as wholehearted engagement in valuable activities and relationships, a life that arises from increasing autonomy to make up one's mind as to the life that is meaningful and worth living.

Pring also considers learning as the defining focus of education. People learn 'facts,' 'concepts', 'principles,' 'skills,' 'attitudes', 'habits' and 'competencies.' (p. 30). People learn how to do things, as well as that something is the case. Teaching is similarly a complex concept to be used to define the purposes of education. 'Teaching habits' is different from 'teaching algebra'; 'teaching how to ride a bicycle' is different from 'teaching how to be virtuous' (p. 34).

Educational discourses are sets of ideas that go together and represent ways in which people use language and think about education. Pring (2015) describes the business discourse as follows:

> Increasingly, therefore, we are being told to think in business terms, defining the product, identifying the process which attains that product, empowering the deliverer (the teacher), and measuring the quality, empowering the client. The product in England is defined in terms of a detailed outcome-related National Curriculum, the 'process' is spelt out in terms of its effectiveness in producing the product. ... Partnerships are created for stakeholders, deliverers and clients to work together in developing the 'effective processes' for producing the 'product' (which incidentally has been defined by someone external to the 'process').
>
> (p. 36)

We, the authors, consider that this is not a helpful way to think of education, as it is linked not only to business but also to manufacturing processes of the Industrial Revolution and is not an up-to-date way of thinking about the world and children. As Pring (2015) points out, it constitutes a new way of thinking about the relationship of teacher and learner. If the product is a measurable target on which performance is audited, where is the place for a struggle to make sense, or a deviant or creative response, or the place of stretching the learning? As Pring (2015) argues, metaphors from business, management, and we would add manufacturing industry do not embody values other than those of efficiency and effectiveness. Thinking about the teacher with a pupil and making sense of a poem, inputs and outputs do not work. The means and end are interrelated.

We have not chosen to define what we think the purpose of education is, as this is something you need to do for yourself. Our own definitions will become clear as you read the book and see the authors' shared values. You need to be thinking ethically about your own practice. Ethics are rules of conduct that people adopt when they act in social contexts. Ethics seek to resolve questions dealing with concepts such as good and evil (McArdle, 2018). We also need to consider internal and external. External morality concerns itself with those values we hold dear as a community of teachers, such as never hitting a child. Internal morality concerns those values we hold dear to ourselves, which underpin our choices of behaviour, such as always greeting every child to ensure they all feel valued.

Freedom can be thought of as both positive and negative. Freedom frequently refers to physical ease, such as freedom from bondage, or grace of movement and frankness of manner. Negative freedom is freedom from barriers. Positive freedom is freedom from self-inhibition of the ability to make desired choices. Barriers to moral choices might be the generally accepted way things are or your lack of confidence to act the way you think is appropriate. Freedom is a state of mind that recognises the positive and negative freedoms and seeks to manage these in order to be free from constraints.

We hope you will have freedom in your thoughts about what is right for learning and teaching for children, for parents/carers, for the school and for yourself.

What we would do to change education

Each chapter in this book has challenge questions. Each of us has chosen to answer some of these questions that are at the end of this chapter, so you can see the diversity and similarity of views we, the authors, hold. These questions are designed to help you to clarify your own opinions and values. Take time to jot down your answers.

Karen, thinking about Scotland, considers the breadth and intent of the school curriculum is to be welcomed with its focus on being interdisciplinary and on cross-curricular learning and the whole child. She thinks that there are not enough schools; in an ideal world, school classes would be smaller and there would be more time and head space for teacher reflection. If Karen was minister for education, she would involve teachers more in consultation and decision making about curriculum and its implementation. Her deeply held beliefs are around the equality and importance of *all* children: The poor and the rich, the bullied and the bully. This latter belief comes from the fact that at primary school Karen was a bully for a short period, and this was because there was trouble at home and she needed help, as did the victim—not blame.

Alison believes that teachers should be given breathing-space to interrogate new initiatives, to reflect on their pedagogical usefulness and potential, and to have a voice at the national level when such nascent initiatives are being discussed. Next, she would re-professionalise our profession: we should not engage in 'initial teacher training,' with its performative undertones. Rather, we should engage in 'initial teacher education, 'encouraging reflection and reflexivity, finding out what our values and belief systems are, what we want the 'difference we make' to be and why; to be informed by research and reading and to be happy questioning findings. 'We teach who we are, and if we don't know who we are, how can we ever make real contact with the children in our classes?' How can they know who we are? This latter belief stems from the fact that so many of Alison's teachers in primary and secondary school shared themselves, their vulnerabilities and their joy and passion for their subject.

John, who is the headteacher of a special school, describes what he would do if he were minister for education in Scotland:

> I would look to implement serious funding to support Additional Support Needs (ASNs) in schools, including mandatory post graduate qualifications for those wishing to become an ASN teacher. While there are many positives to Scotland's Getting It Right for Every Child (GIRFEC)[1] approach, it can often fall flat in schools due to chronic underfunding, staff confidence in teaching those with additional support needs and access to quality professional development. To support genuine inclusion, not integration, I believe every school needs access to a well-trained ASN teacher with an expectation and time to continually develop their knowledge and practice through collaboration with families, health professionals and academic research.
>
> I would implement a career progression and professional standards for Pupils Support Assistants, who have committed to relevant training and have skills to support those with significant learning needs. Finally, I would ensure that any new schools being built are carefully designed to support inclusion and pupil wellbeing.

Penny says, I would budget for free school meals for all children by providing extra financing (as in Greater London); provide a budget for all schools to deliver free extracurricular activities, with trained external staff, which would cover a wide variety of activities; include sufficient time for all teachers and support staff to be able to access training for pastoral care; and possibly budget for a pastoral team in every school.

Learning points

1. Values make a difference to the child's experience at school;
2. It is important to make explicit the values that underpin what we do as educators;
3. Teachers are good at what they do because of who they are;
4. Knowing the purpose of education is critical to understanding the context in which we teach, and our own understanding of the purpose of education will influence our practice;
5. Values can be defined as broad preferences concerning appropriate courses of action or outcomes.

Challenge questions

1. Who was your favourite teacher at school and why?
2. Who was your least favourite teacher and why?
3. Do you teach like your favourite teacher?
4. What do you think is right about education in this country today?
5. What is wrong with education in this country now?
6. If you were the minister for education, what would you change?
7. What are your deeply held beliefs about education? Where did these come from?

Note

1. Getting it right for every child (GIRFEC) is the Scottish government's commitment to provide all children, young people and their families with the right support at the right time. This is so that every child and young person in Scotland can reach their full potential. They want all children and young people to live in an equal society that enables them to flourish, to be treated with kindness, dignity and respect, and to have their rights upheld at all times.

References

Carr, D. (2003). *Making sense of education: An introduction to the philosophy and theory of education and teaching*. Routledge, Abingdon, UK.

Dworkin, G. (2007). Unprincipled ethics. In R. Shafer-Landau (Ed.), *Ethical theory: An anthology*. Blackwell Publishing, Malden MA.

Malik, K. (2015). *The quest for a moral compass: A global history of ethics*. Atlantic Books, London, UK.

McArdle, K. (2018). *Freedom research in education: Becoming an autonomous researcher*. Palgrave Macmillan, Cham, Switzerland.

McArdle, K., Hurrell, A., & Munoz Martinez, Y. (2013). What makes teachers good at what they do? In J. McNiff (Ed.), *The axiological model in value and virtue in practice-based research*. September Books, Poole, Dorset, UK.

Orsi, F. (2015). *Value theory*. Bloomsbury Ethics, London, UK.

Pring, T. (2004). *Philosophy of education: Aims, theory, commons sense and research*. Continuum Books, London, UK.

Pring, T. (2015). *Philosophy of educational R=research*. Bloomsbury, London, UK.

Rachels, J. (2007). Ethical egoism. In R. Shafer-Landau (Ed.), *Ethical theory: An anthology*. Blackwell Publishing, Malden, MA.

Ransome, P. (2013). *Ethics and values in social research*. Palgrave Macmillan, Hampshire, UK.

White, J. (2003). Autonomy, human flourishing and the curriculum. *Journal of the Philosophy of Education* 40(3).

Van Manen, M. (2007). Phenomenology of practice. *Phenomenology of Practice* 1, 11-30.

3 Why we do what we do, or vocation

Introduction

You might like to jot down your answers to the following two questions before you start reading.

1. Why did you choose teaching as a career?
2. What is it about you that makes you want to teach?

More about Karen's teachers: Molly was one of Karen's favourite teachers at school. She was a maths teacher in secondary school and spent considerable time making sure that everyone, yes everyone, understood. She was always calm and kind and had no favourites; everyone felt favourite. Even the boys, who used to misbehave in other classes, were good in her classes as they knew she cared and would take her time. Molly cared about teaching and was determined everyone should learn. She took pride in what she did. She saw teaching as her vocation, enabling us as a class to navigate the world of numbers. She cared about our futures. She lived her values.

A vocation?

Teaching is often referred to as a vocation, but teaching as a vocation sounds rather old-fashioned now. Molly was a teacher a long time ago, but we think a vocation is still relevant. We wish to suggest a vocation, or why we do what we do, is important at different levels for all teachers, young and old, beginning and experienced. Vocation defines our philosophy and hence practice and the approaches we choose to adopt for teaching, so we consider it is worth valuing highly. Not all teachers have the same vocation or a vocation to the same depth in terms of its influence on practice. Vocation is perhaps a little daunting to the beginning teacher–almost religious, suggesting she or he has a moral commitment to 'do good in society'–but we shall argue that it is different for different people.

When the four authors of this book think of a teacher with a strong vocation, we think of a teacher who is both committed and caring: Committed to the purposes of the profession and caring with the children. Estola et al. (2003) wonder if the revival of the idea of vocation is a nostalgic longing for the past in the chaotic present of many societies. We suggest that vocation is not a longing for the past; vocation has never gone away, it is just how we talk about it that is different. We now talk more often about values and beliefs. Estola et al. (2003) use the term 'vocation' and give the following rather dry definitions:

- An ethical orientation or dedication;
- A response to a call by the children and orientation of pedagogy to respond to this;
- A career based on vocation.

We shall return to the ethical orientation shortly. The 'call' by children refers to the nature of teaching as a 'calling' or job choice, and this puts the child at the centre of the profession. Alison thinks of the smile a child has when she or he learns something important as being the calling. The reference to a career based on vocation links to healthcare and religion and other professions often referred to as vocations, where there are expectations that you will work hard, be good at what you do and will do your best.

Dewey has interesting ideas about vocation. Higgins (2005), in discussing Dewey's ideas, says the teacher is frequently addressed as if they have no life of their own. They are defined by the role they play in a classroom. The individual's personal biography is overlooked. We would argue that this is very much not the case. Yes, children can be surprised to see their teacher in the supermarket, but everyone remembers who was a good teacher and who was a bad one as they grow up. We would argue that the personal biography of the teacher determines what kind of teacher she or he is. We shall return to this quite often in this book.

We are of the opinion that it is largely who one is that characterizes the vocation and hence practice. Vocation is something the individual has, but it is also collective, meaning we are part of a profession. It is not to do with organisations we are members of or with which we are registered. We consider it links to Wenger's (2009) notion of a community of practice, groups of people who share a concern or a passion for something they do and learn how to do it better as they interact regularly. There is something important about being passionate and something about a commitment to learning that defines vocation for us.

In discussing healthcare, Ballatt and Campling (2011) refer to vocation as conveying a sense that one's chosen profession is more than just a job. It suggests that professionals are deeply privileged to have the opportunity and expertise to be involved (in healthcare). This implies a certain degree of gratitude that one can contribute to the profession, which, we suggest, often links to the motivation we have to teach (Ballatt & Campling, 2011). There is also a hint of altruism, the desire to do something that makes a difference to others' lives, which teaching clearly does. Vocation is deeply personal and is linked to values; altruism is a value.

Inspectors, headteachers, parents and the social, economic and cultural communities all have an impact on what education is like, but the individual experience for the child is in the lap of the teacher and their values to a great extent. So, values can be very individual as well as social and cultural.

Before we started to write this chapter, Alison and I thought hard about vocation and what it meant for each of us. Alison defines vocation in the following terms:

- Willing resilience/perseverance to reach one's goal;
- Vocation is felt but rarely articulated;
- Could I possibly do anything else to be fulfilled?

- Keep going in the face of ridicule and belittlement;
- Exploration and excitement even when the way ahead seems bleak.

Alison saw her vocation in terms of her motivation, her personal fulfilment and her behaviour, relating to the ability to carry on when the work is difficult. She also, very importantly, referred to the way she felt. Values are often inexplicit and only appear by making us feel uncomfortable when we have a hint that we have done something wrong.

Karen saw her vocation quite differently in terms of:

- A strong commitment to her profession;
- A commitment on the basis that it (the profession) embraces the right things to do;
- A profession within which she can live with herself;
- A need to do the best for everyone;
- A profession for which she has a passion.

Once again feelings mattered. Karen needs to be able to live with herself, so she has set standards for her behaviour that are largely implicit. Her vocation has dimensions of the values of equality and the need to do the best for everyone. She believes in the profession as it embraces, for her, the right things to do in education. So vocation is multifaceted and linked to one's beliefs about the way the world should be. It embraces feelings, it embraces behaviour and how we think about ourselves as individuals and as teachers.

A challenge John came across particularly in middle management roles is leading change in pedagogy, for example moving to synthetic phonic programmes or play-based pedagogies. This had a devaluing effect on those who have taught to a system, usually successfully for years. When an experienced teacher was told, 'we are moving to a different pedagogy,' I have heard 'so what you are saying is everything I have done over the last twenty years is wrong?' or 'I have successfully taught children to read; why do I need to change how I teach?' This was due to the school as a whole not valuing the need to keep up to date with current research and rigorously reflecting on practice. The first step to any change is ensuring we have co-created, shared values.

It is common to discuss shared values, but we are of the view that these are particular to the individual. Two teachers may share the value of believing all children are equal, but how this affects their behaviour to the individual child may be very different, as explained earlier. Values are also not separate from each other and are not one-dimensional. The teacher who brings in breakfast for hungry children is manifesting a complex of beliefs or values about education, their role in education and the learning needs of the child. We suggest your values are determined by your upbringing, the culture of the society you live, and by your experience, in particular of your own education.

Our upbringing determines many things linked to values, not least how we value other people and, therefore, the children with whom we work. The society we live in determines how education is structured and how we perceive education. Karen has worked with Aboriginal people in Australia who live their traditional life. They did not originally have systems of schools but, yes, learning took place in all its complexity. School is an invention of society, and learning takes place in and out of school, as we all know, and how we value this learning is determined socially. Who says that learning in school is better, and if so why? Our culture affects how we learn. Do we value facts and memory more than understanding and problem solving? If so, we would teach by rote, like people do in other countries. Finally, our own experience of education will have an impact on what we value and what we believe works in education.

Identity

We believe that identity is inseparable from values. A definition of identity as story, derived from Clandinin and Caine (2013), provides a definition that we like.

> Story is a portal through which a person enters the world and by which their experience of the world is interpreted and made personally meaningful.
>
> (p. 542)

Stories we tell of our lives reveal who we think we are and who we want to be. If you have stories you tell about your days at school, you might like to think of what the stories say about you and your understanding of school. Karen remembers her first day at school, and what remains with her is her terror at not being able to find the peg on which to hang her coat, which had her name on it. The terror was about fitting in and belonging as well as the need to be able to manage the new systems that go with school and its expectations of behaviour.

Our identity determines our behaviour or the 'self we live by' (Holstein & Gubrium, 2000). Questions about self arise frequently throughout our lives.

- Who are you?
- Who am I?
- What kind of people are we?
- What have we done?
- Who will we become?
- What do we really think?
- How do we feel?
- How do we behave?

(Derived from Holstein & Gubrium, 2000, p. 84)

The answer to each of these questions determines the kind of teacher we are or shall be. Another way of thinking about identity is thinking of the 'self we live by.'

Foucault (1977) explains that it was not until the last few centuries in Western Europe that people were seen as individuals with all the social, legal and moral dimensions that go with this. Before this, people were largely undifferentiated from the groups and activities with which they were associated. There was arguably, we suggest, a stronger emphasis on community and self rather than the individual and self. How we conceptualise self is highly subjective. We engage, say Holstein and Gubrium (2000), in structuring our lives so they appear meaningful, organised and coherent. So, in a sense we create ourselves using our experience and the resources available to us to become someone. It is not simply that our experiences make us who we are, but the meaning we attach to those experiences colours us.

Karen's parents were divorced when she was a teenager and she reacted completely differently from her sister, who was in the same situation. The meaning Karen put on the circumstances and the self she created from the experience was quite different from her sister's.

We constantly revisit the same experiences, and our meaning may change as we get older. The meaning you put on your experiences will affect the kind of teacher you are or become. For example, your experiences might affect how you trust people, and how you trust people will affect how you work with others.

Defining education

What we think of ourselves, and ourselves in relation to others, affects what we think about education—what we think it is, who we think it is for and how we enact these beliefs. It is not easy to find a definition for education, as it is for the term 'game'. We all know what a game is, and we all recognise one when we see it, but trying to find a definition that covers all games such as cricket, chess, patience and monopoly is impossible. You might know from experience what you consider to be bad education, but good education is harder to explain. Peters (1966) points out that to educate someone implies some sort of achievement that is worthwhile on the part of the pupil. He also suggests it is the intentional bringing about of a desirable state of mind in a "morally unobjectionable manner" (p. 27). This latter is to differentiate it from brainwashing.

Sometimes people think of education in terms of gardening. This embraces nurturing and cultivating, through application of some kind of effort to make the plants (children) grow. This has been criticised for implying that, without the nurturing, the plants would not grow or children would not learn, but we think it a good analogy, as plants do want to grow themselves but grow better with someone helping or watering them, as long as they get the nurturing right. (See Chapter 11 on Nurturing)

The purpose of education is also tricky to define. Some people think the purpose is to equip people for suitable jobs to grow the economy. We think it also has an individual and community function. We think it has a broader purpose than just jobs and the economy. The adult needs to contribute to the community in many ways such as a family member, a volunteer, as well as a hard-working contributor to the economy. We also think the adult needs to be confident, resilient and, yes, they should have the potential for happiness.

We need to also think about what education consists of. It is not just about skills. It also consists of knowledge and understanding. Frequently it is considered to embrace attributes like being conscientious. So education may be argued to consist of three things: First, its matter; second, its manner; and third, its cognitive perspective (Peters, 1966). In fact, it consists of a synthesis of all three. Next, we need to think of 'teaching.' All sorts of activities count as teaching, but what they have in common is the intention that learning occurs, a connection between what the teacher does and what the pupil is intended to learn, and some connection between what the teacher says and does and the understanding of the pupil (Pring, 2006).

But as Pring (2006) says, this a rather desiccated definition of what a teacher does. Teachers are initiated into a practice that has its own value and conducts, which are frequently implicit. 'But they embody a commitment to helping young people to learn those things which are judged to be worthwhile' (p. 16). This means that teaching is a moral enterprise as the teacher needs to judge what is worthwhile, which Pring defines as the 'initiation of (usually) young people into a worthwhile way of seeing the world, of experiencing it, of relating to others in a more human and understanding way' (p. 18).

If you have been thinking that the curriculum guides teaching, Pring (2006) has an interesting comment to make on this.

> I wish to argue that what makes sense of the curriculum in educational terms is that it is the forum or the vehicle through which young people are enabled to explore seriously (in the light of evidence and argument) what it is to be human. And such as exploration has no end. That is why teaching should be regarded as a moral practice.
>
> (p. 25)

We shall talk more about curriculum in Chapter 9: Things, place and time for children. The link of moral judgement to practice is crucial in our opinion. What we believe influences what we do. If we believe all children are equal, then we might struggle to overcome some of the injustices that affect children from a disadvantaged background. We need to know what we believe so that we can see how this influences our behaviour, or see how our behaviour reflects what we believe. It used to be common to seek to clarify values using games of values clarification. Which person would you rescue first from an accident, the pregnant woman or the elderly gentleman who used to be a doctor? These are not, we suggest, terribly helpful in finding out what we believe in a practical context. We believe instead in reflection and reflexivity. There terms will reappear in the book as we think they are so important.

Reflection and reflexivity

'Reflection' is a much-contested term (McArdle, 2018). It often is used to describe the informal discussion of an incident in the staff room. We think it needs to be more critical than that. Bolton (2010) describes reflection in the following terms.

> Reflection is in-depth review of events either alone – say in a journal – or with critical support with a supervisor group. The reflector attempts to work out what has happened, what they thought or felt about it, who was involved, when and where, what these others might have experienced and thought and felt about it from their own perspective.
>
> (p. 7)

It is our experience that reflective practice in a busy environment can fall by the wayside. Reflective practice is, however, the main means of dealing with complexity and change. This is because it gives us the space to process complexity and to synthesise ideas, so that we can make good judgements about our action, responding as best we can to the complexity that surrounds us, and use all our ways of knowing in forming opinions and making choices.

Fook and Gardner (2007) define the method of critical reflection that we believe can make a difference to both society and the individual's practice. Clearly, reflection is about thinking, but it is more than this. It involves a deeper look at the assumptions on which, thinking, action and emotions are based. The key points are the understanding of self in a social context, challenging assumptions and linking a changed way of thinking to changed actions.

Why we do what we do, or vocation 27

Reflective practice has the potential to effect change in society as well as in the individual. Our changed actions can affect the world in which we live. It is in principle about unearthing taken-for-granted assumptions.

Here we give two examples to show reflection and reflexivity. The first is of reflection between Karen and Clare (derived from McArdle et al., 2020).

Karen: 'I ran a group training session on learning and teaching the new curriculum. It was supposed to have ten people but only four turned up and I felt it was rather flat and unexciting. The people reported to the organiser, who evaluated that it was good but it troubles me now two weeks after the event that I did not make it as lively and exciting as it could have been.'

Clare: What is it about you that requires every event to be 'lively and exciting'? It seems that the participants found it fine.

Karen: I like to do a good job for everyone.

Clare: But they said you did do a good job. Why are you putting your opinion above the opinion of the participants?

Karen: Fair point. I guess I am used to doing these workshops and consider myself to be a bit of a whizz on this topic.

Clare: How about using the feedback more explicitly and judging yourself in this context rather than according to your own terms.

Karen: Thanks. I shall do this next time.

In this short piece, Clare was challenging Karen and helped her to see that her opinion was unbalanced; most importantly, Clare found a way to lead to a different action in a similar situation. Often reflection is about assumptions, and these are based on deeply held beliefs about the world and self in the world. The previous conversation could have taken a different and equally valid path using reflexivity after Karen outlined the problem to Clare, as outlined in the following example.

Clare: What is it about you, Karen, that requires that every session is perfect? The participants said it was fine. Are you a perfectionist?

Karen: Well, I suppose I set high standards for myself all the time.

Clare: Why is that?

Karen: Well, I guess I always want to be the best at what I do.

Clare: Where does that come from?

Karen: Well, I suppose I've always been like that since I was a child. My parents had high, very high expectations of what I should achieve in everything, and I guess that lives with me now.

Clare: Well, it clearly causes you some stress, as you are concerned two weeks after the event about something that was good but not perfect. How about accepting 'good' and working with the participants to see if they indeed missed what you think was missing?

It is important to reflect on action, but in a way that challenges and is not too safe. There is a place for safe conversations, but these are not necessarily reflection or reflexivity for learning. Reflexivity asks critical questions rather than reviewing or reacting. It challenges our taken-for-granted assumptions. Dean (2014) refers to reflexivity as metacognition: Thinking about thinking, learning about learning.

Learning points

1. The concept of vocation has never gone away; it is just how we talk about it that is different.
2. Vocation defines one's philosophy and hence practice and the approaches we choose to adopt for teaching.
3. Teaching is a profession that shares a concern, a passion for something we do, and we learn how to do it better as we interact regularly.
4. The society we live in determines how education is structured and how we perceive education.
5. Critical thinking about what we do and the impact we have on the children we teach is at the heart of professional development.

Challenge questions

1. Who do you enjoy talking to about school? Why this person and not others?
2. What do you think is worth learning?
3. What are the worthwhile ways of pursuing this?
4. Can you think of a time when you learnt about learning?
5. Or thought about thinking?
6. Or reflected about reflection?
7. How would you describe your vocation or reasons for being teacher?

The process of reflection is, we hope, built into this book so that you will be thinking about yourself as a teacher as you are reading it. Go back to your answers to the first two questions at the start of this chapter: What do your answers say about the reasons you are a teacher? In the next chapter, we are going to focus on the importance of building trust with the children, colleagues and the wider community of parents and carers.

References

Ballatt, J., & Campling, P. (2011). *Intelligent kindness: Reforming the culture of healthcare*. RCPsych Publications, London.
Bolton, G. (2010). *Reflective practice: Writing and professional development* (4th ed.). Sage, London.
Clandinin, D.J., & Caine, V. (2013). Narrative inquiry. In *Reviewing qualitative research in the social sciences* (pp. 166-179). Routledge, London.
Dean, C. (2014). How the process of doctoral enquiry developed my openness and teaching. presentation. *4th International Conference on Values and Virtues in Practice Based Research*, July 21-3, York St John University, York, UK.

Estola, E., Erkkila, R., & Syrja, L. (2003). A moral voice of vocation in teachers' narratives. *Teachers and Teaching* 9(3), 239-256.

Fook, J., & Gardner, F. (2007). *Practising critical reflection: A resource handbook*, Open University Press, Maidenhead, UK.

Foucault. (1977). In S. Hall (Ed.), *Foucault: Power, knowledge and discourse theory and practice: A reader*. (2001). Penguin Books, London.

Higgins, C. (2005). Dewey's conception of vocation: Existential, aesthetic, and educational implications for teachers. *Journal of Curriculum Studies* 37(4), 441-446.

Holstein, J.A., & Gubrium, J.F. (2000). *The self we live by: Narrative identity in a postmodern world*. Oxford University Press, Oxford, UK.

McArdle, K. (2018). *Freedom research in education: Becoming an autonomous researcher*. Palgrave Macmillan, Cham, Switzerland.

McArdle, K., Briggs, S., Garrett, E., & McKay, C. (2020). *The impact of community work: How to gather evidence*. Policy Press, London.

Peters, R.S. (1966). *Ethics and education*. Routledge, London.

Pring, R. (2006). *Philosophy of education: Aims, theory, commons sense and research*. Continuum, London.

Wenger, E. (2009). Communities of practice: The key to knowledge strategy. In E. L. Lesser, M. A. Fontaine, & J. A. Slusher (Eds.), *Knowledge and communities* (pp. 3-20). Routledge.

PART TWO

In this section of the book, we discuss the values and virtues that we consider to be important to good teachers. We consider learning to be incremental for educators, and we do not expect you to be working on all of the virtues at the same time. You might like to dip in and out of this book for this part, or you may wish to read this whole section of the book and return to important chapters later. You may consider we have left out values and virtues that you think are important, and we would be interested to hear what these are.

4 Trust and resilience

Choose to be kind, friends, choose to be kind:
Wherever you are, on or off line, see what you find?
In the street, in your classroom, kindness glows and it shines
At home or away, winter, spring, night or day.
Today you know for sure you won't need a reminder.
When faced with a choice it's kind of better to be kinder!

(Jackie Kay, 2017, p. 11; originally published in *Ten Poems of Kindness, Volume One* [Candlestick Press, 2017], used by kind permission of the author).

This verse from a poem invites us to think about kindness to others as something we can choose. Showing kindness is closely linked to creating trust. We have devoted a complete chapter to kindness. Trust, in this chapter, is about relationships and attitudes. We have an informal definition of trust that we enjoy – *the promise of a good future relationship, all things being equal*. Trust is about relationships in our definition and has a predictive quality for future behaviour. The opposite is distrust or mistrust. This definition implies certain past and current behaviours, too:

- Have faith in;
- Put or place one's trust in;
- Pin one's hopes/faith on;
- Have confidence in;
- Believe on;
- Rely on;
- Depend on;
- Count on;
- Be sure of;
- Be convinced by;
- Swear by;
- Confide in.

(https://www.dictionary.com/browse/trust (accessed 1 February 2024)

DOI: 10.4324/9781032678283-6

The opposites of trust are mistrust and distrust, which are clearly linked to feelings of suspicion, fear and anxiety.

All of the foregoing implies strong emotions; trust implies a certain allowing yourself to let go, with a feeling of confidence that someone cares. The link between the foregoing phrases and deeply held values is apparent, with the words 'belief,' 'faith' and 'hope,' for example.

Trust is crucial between pupils and teachers and, of course, parents. Trust has a relationship to behaviours such as fairness, caring, reliability, predictability, continuity and honesty or authenticity, which are just a few of the qualities that good teachers need. This is to be sensitive to pupils' feelings and is linked to good classroom behaviour—not expecting the pupils simply to be 'good' or 'quiet,' but allowing pupils to be wrong, to take risks and try new things. Trust is not found or formed in one day. It is how we 'stay in the conversation' that matters (Centre for Courage & Renewal, 2018, p. 83).

Trust with pupils

> Teacher credibility is the students' belief that they can learn from a particular teacher because, the teacher is believable, convincing, and capable of persuading students that they can be successful. If a teacher is not perceived as credible, the students just turn off.
> This credibility is a function of beliefs about teachers' trust, competence, passion for their subject, and desire for the students to learn in their class.
>
> (Hattie, 2023, p. 226)

The quotation from Hattie is about credibility of teachers and its importance for children's learning and behaviour in class. Trust is linked to competence and passion for their subject. Trust in the classroom is also about relationships and the opposite of ruling by fear. Bruney (2012) suggests teachers should be prepared to share their own strengths, weaknesses and personal experiences with their students to connect with and establish meaningful relationships with them. Bruney (2012) says children will share who they are with us if we share who we are with them.

Bruney also discusses authenticity of teacher behaviour, describing how children spot quickly if teachers are not truly interested in them and what they say. A teacher Bruney describes claims that once her students established that their lives and feelings were important to her and that she valued their points of view, presence and contribution in class, they would thereby value her presence in return (2012, p. 24).

Attitude to learning is also crucial in building trust. We already mentioned competence and passion. Bruney (2012) describes Jan's and Jade's approach to learning and teaching:

> Jan's goal is to foster intrinsic motivation and self-confidence in her students by genuinely caring about their overall well-being and academic success. Jade states that 'if you are an authentic person, then you believe in yourself. If you believe in yourself then you will believe in others.' It is important that teachers highlight student strength and help them to build on their weakness. I have learned that if students are constantly reminded of and know what they are good at doing, they could use these positive traits to build on their weaker areas.
>
> (p. 25)

Building trust is important, and it is about finding a balanced relationship. The teacher is not a friend or a parent but may have some of the positive qualities of these relationships. Building trust is illustrated by Alison's case study of her teaching in a secondary school context:

Am I doing okay, Miss?

James was 12 and recently enrolled into S1 (year 11) from a different high school from which he had been excluded. He was exuberant, bright, confident and cheeky – already popular with his peers and quite disengaged from any aspect of the formal curriculum, especially my aspect of the curriculum, French. He was soon on behaviour cards for all his classes, frequently in detention and the hot topic of conversation in the staff room.

But I liked him. I've always liked that rebellious side of a teenager. but his opening remark of "I'm not f***ing doing this, and you can't make me!" couldn't go without some kind of reaction. The other children in the class knew that one of our agreed rules was that bad language wasn't needed inside the classroom since I would never use bad language with them. They were looking at me, waiting for me to say something and James was also looking at me, waiting for a confrontation that he (and I) knew he would win. I had to be predictable, consistent and fair to everyone, hard though that was at times. 'You're right,' I said. 'I can't make you. You can leave if you want to, but we were just going to talk about the school trip to Brittany coming up next Easter and what we would want to do there. I was hoping you would want to go. ... Oh, and James, don't use that language. Thank you!'

He stayed. I don't think that was down to me. The other children in the class were all excited about the trip and just relieved at that moment in time, I think, that they and I would continue our chat about plans for Brittany without having a fiery confrontation played out before them.

But I know that was only the starting point of trying to win his trust in me. His home life was difficult; his father was in prison, and his mum struggled to make ends meet, holding down three jobs. He was too young to be responsible for his two siblings, and he resented the responsibility with no acceptable way of letting off steam. School learning was not valued at home, and learning a foreign language "was of no use at all because you'll never need it!"

But he was a fast learner and deserved all the praise I gave him (and the rest of the class) when efforts had been made to participate in activities, to work with others in group tasks, to smile and to laugh when a joke was made. We had a favourite-word-of-the-week moment at the end of each week. One Friday, James volunteered the following:

> "My favourite word was concombre, miss! What does it mean?" he asked. I said, "Cucumber" and he burst out laughing. "Aw that's funny. I hate cucumber but I love the word!" To hear him laugh was just a joy.

And then at the end of one double period on a soggy afternoon, he put his hand up and called me over, and very quietly he asked, 'This is hard, miss. Am I doing okay?' My answer was a simple 'Oui' with a big smile.

Over time, James and I became 'friends', potential adversaries at times, but consistency, kindness and understanding seemed to go a long way for us. And it was reciprocated as well. He was doing okay.

Effective schooling relies of course on co-operation and support between home and school. This is the case, for example, with home reinforcement of school decisions about home learning activity, as well as broad expectations that there will be home encouragement for, and interest in, children's school success (Forsyth et al., 2005). Parents can also enter a relationship of trust with teachers. This, however, is complicated by the child being an additional source of information about whether the teacher is trustworthy (Adams & Forsyth, 2009). In the USA, patterns of school success and survival appear to hinge on a variety of contextual conditions, including parental wealth, parental trust, teacher efficacy beliefs, teacher trust and school structure (Forsyth et al., 2005). Accordingly, parental and teacher trust is important. The whole system of the school needs to be working on a model of mutual trust.

Respect for multicultural parents and family

Working with children from a variety of different cultures, countries and social backgrounds provides us with the valuable opportunity to enrich our own lives, as well as broaden our perspectives on life. It is always important to respect and understand different cultures because it helps to create a more inclusive and harmonious society. Just as it is important to build successful and valuable relationships with all parents and carers, it is important to understand and respect parents and carers from a wide variety of different cultures. For example, if there is a language barrier, it is important to recognise this, and if possible use a person on site to translate, or use a technical device to enable clear understanding. It is also essential to be well informed about the variety of different celebrations and places of worship throughout the year, which will enable respect and understanding of other cultures and religions.

Penny explains one example of this was when a Sikh child she taught wanted to attend his Gudwara for Vaisakhi. It was important for him to observe this religious celebration, so he did. Mum was very grateful and showed her appreciation by bringing food for the staff and class, which they heartily appreciated. Another example of developing strong relations with parents from different cultures is understanding aspects of the Muslim faith. It is important to understand the significance of fasting and prayer during Ramadan. Ramadan and Eid are very significant times in the Muslim calendar, which should be recognised in school. Some Muslim children attend daily mosque after school throughout the school year, which can have an impact on homework or after-school activities. Therefore, gaining the trust of parents ensures better communication and cooperation for the child, and if we understand and respect a child's background, we should always move forward.

School can also make a considerable impact on the lives of some parents by helping them enlist in learning English and enrolling in English classes. This then enables parents to understand more about their child's education.

Sometimes trust can be challenged when the wellbeing of the child is at risk and safeguarding is necessary. Software can be used to manage information linked to safeguarding. Naturally we worry about the ethics of data being held about children online, perhaps even following them into adulthood, but Penny finds the advantages outweigh the disadvantages:

> The safeguarding online system we use in school has enabled me to receive protected information regarding some children I have taught over the years. The advantages of

the system are many. I feel they outweigh the disadvantages, which are that it can be time consuming. It has particularly helped me to ensure continuity of care, both in and out of the classroom setting, enabling me to teach certain children with added background information recorded chronologically and professionally. Reading and recording information is always outside teaching time and can mean following up immediately. However, the welfare of a child is paramount when teaching and caring for a child in your care.

Elsie (not real name) had been placed under Child Protection measures, because of an accumulation of family domestic problems and, more importantly, had stopped eating. There had also been a lack of parental engagement with outside services. Therefore, the child had been fast tracked to see a child mental health worker, a dietitian and a family support worker from school. As teacher, although sad I found this very useful to learn, as it provided me with more background to the way Elsie behaved with peers, as well as in class. She was withdrawn, lacked motivation, was often late to school and was also often tired, although she was very happy to be in school.

Because I saw Elsie on a daily basis throughout the year, it was helpful for me to understand all the procedures put in place, as soon as they were enacted, especially when I was so concerned for her wellbeing. Much of the chronological information recorded on the software system included parental behaviour at welfare meetings; parental non-engagement with outside agencies; and medical information, which enabled me to view Elsie's activities and interactions with other children in a more informed light.

The eventual outcome for Elsie was very positive after extensive support and collaboration between school, outside agencies and parents. Using the software enabled me (and the pastoral team) to record important, relevant information, as well as view up-to-date ongoing information. This thereby helped to support a more positive future for Elsie.

During the Covid-19 pandemic and 'lockdown' which closed schools, the system was particularly useful for teachers or professionals, who were able to monitor those children who were causing safeguarding concerns. Any teacher who was linked to a child whilst at home during lockdown could view and then voice their concerns. Home visits followed, and the children were then invited to come to school instead of staying at home. This provided a good safeguarding measure for all of the children and enabled all staff involved to understand the best way forward for each child.

Resilience

Thinking about safeguarding the child, we also need to think about safeguarding ourselves. Reflecting on the many influences at all levels described in the three chapters so far and drawing on our own experience of teachers and teaching, we, the authors, found ourselves thinking about tiredness, low morale, overload, curriculum tyranny and social isolation. In short, those of us with long experience felt that some teachers had become increasingly disempowered over the last 20 to 30 years in the UK. This, we consider, was a product of the role of the teacher extending to embrace not just teaching and learning but also counselling, therapy, social work and parenthood, and also many increasing social demands being placed upon the teacher. So, we ask, what is teaching like today, and how do we cope?

The world workforce of 80 million teachers is indeed changing. Hattie (2023) cites Ingersoll et al. (2014), who describe the trends in the teacher workforce from the 1980s in the USA, showing the overall workforce is larger, older, greener (i.e., more beginning teachers), more female, more diverse, and academically okay. People are less likely to stay a teacher, are trained to use online methods, start keen and hungry (more willing to embrace professional standards and engage with other teachers) and are pay deprived. Hattie (2023) suggests this is emulated in many of the Organisation for Economic Co-operation and Development (OECD) Western countries.

The disempowerment of teachers is also, we suggest, a product of insufficient resources. For example, the number of pupils with additional support needs (ASNs or special educational needs and disabilities (SEND) and with complex needs has increased year by year in the UK, with few additional resources to cope with the increasing demand. Poverty of children's families places additional demands on teachers, again with limited additional resources. Similarly, lack of involvement of teachers in a plethora of new educational policies can lead to unworkable situations that teachers must seek to make workable in the classroom. We consider many things could be done to alleviate this situation, not least additional funding to support areas of complex need. Pastoral care for teachers is vital, and we consider more emphasis and time for continuing professional development (CPD) is important to allow cross-classroom and cross-school sharing.

Resilience for the individual teacher is accordingly significant, and this can begin with us holding onto what makes teaching at its best such a rewarding job. Fundamental to teaching are relationships and trust. Mutual respect with children is desirable along with valuing creativity and imagination and the joy of learning with pupils. You will have your own reasons for being a teacher, and it is important for resilience to hold onto these if you find yourself feeling disempowered.

"Resilience focuses on recovery, the ability to rebound from stress, a capacity to regain equilibrium quickly and to return to an initial state of health" and we would add a state of well-being (Reich, Zautra & Hall, 2010, p. xi). We define wellbeing as living a life of value for self and others.

Grotberg (1995) devised a model for thinking about children's resilience, and we think it can apply to adults too. It is a very simple model of 'I have, I am, I can.'

Examples Grotberg gives for the child are as follows:

I HAVE

People around me I trust and who love me, no matter what;
People who set limits for me so I know when to stop before there is danger or trouble;
People who show me how to do things right by the way they do things;
People who want me to learn to do things on my own;
People who help me when I am sick, in danger or need to learn.

I AM

A person people can like and love;
Glad to do nice things for others and show my concern;

Respectful of myself and others;
Willing to be responsible for what I do;
Sure things will be all right.

I CAN

Talk to others about things that frighten or bother me;
Find ways to solve problems that I face;
Control myself when I feel like doing something not right or dangerous;
Figure out when it is a good time to talk to someone or to take action;
Find someone to help me when I need it.

(Grotberg, 1995, Introduction)

Not all these factors are needed for resilience, says Grotberg, but one is not enough. We need a combination of resources. For an adult they may *have* support and coping strategies. For 'I am' they may be confident and committed to teaching. For 'I can' there are colleagues they may *have* and family and friends they *can* talk to. The 'I have' factors are the external supports and resources that promote resilience. The 'I am' factors are the internal, personal strengths. The 'I can' factors are the social and interpersonal skills.

Support of colleagues is very important to resilience, and trust is the foundation for good relationships. Trust in a workplace with colleagues takes time to create, and at the heart of trust is self-awareness and socio-emotional intelligence (Center for Courage & Renewal, 2018). Relational trust is a specific form of trust that arises from relationships between people in organisations or communities. It comes from our inner perceptions and interpretation of others' behaviour and motives (Center for Courage & Renewal, 2018). It may be worth noting, as an aside, that in schools where trust between teachers was strong pupils' test scores improved (Center for Courage & Renewal, 2018, p. 77).

There are four lenses of relational trust. We observe and interpret the behaviour of others in a split second through the interplay of the lenses of respect, personal regard, competence and integrity (Bryk & Schneider, 2002). Respect involves honouring the role each person plays in the school and recognising mutual dependencies. Personal regard simply means taking care to notice others and their opinions. Competence means valuing and being aware of the talents of others. Finally, integrity is explained by the Center for Courage & Renewal (2018) as there being consistency between what people say and do. 'We sense integrity when a person's work appears to be guided by a deeper moral-ethical commitment … In schools, teachers or principals demonstrate integrity when they act with the best interests of children at heart' … (p. 81).

Trust with colleagues builds resilience and is the opposite of a fear-based culture. Davies (2021, p. 36) argues that there are four preconditions for a trust-based school culture:

- The ability to speak openly;
- The ability to be adult;
- The ability to see failure as an opportunity to learn;
- The ability to give and receive robust, curious feedback.

The trust-based culture in turn leads to outcomes of collaboration, upskilling one another, improved teaching, and wellbeing (p. 37).

The ability to speak openly can be blocked by many factors, such as a hierarchy in the school. Hierarchy may be linked to perceived worth, wisdom and power. Having clearly defined roles is important to schools, but undefined hierarchy or not-spoken-about hierarchy is a huge barrier to communication and therefore mutual support (Davies, 2021).

The ability to be an adult is important; each person needs to take responsibility for their work and to be proactive, accountable and solutions-focused (Davies, 2021). We would add being child/children focused at all times. In short, teachers need to be empowered in their roles to be free to make decisions and be supported.

Failure at work is a negative concept for self and others. We prefer to think of being malleable and able to improve at all times while recognising a job well done. If, as Davies (2021) says, we are a victim to things going awry, then failure takes on a sinister role. If teachers believe they can change, grow and learn, then this will affect how they treat others and how others treat them.

The ability to give and receive feedback is crucial to being a good and improving teacher. Davies suggests compassion, care and expertise in giving feedback, and we would add sensitivity and knowledge of the person who is receiving feedback.

Reflecting on our own practice, we find that resilience is compromised through lack of time for reflection and, in particular, shared reflection, which itself builds trust. We are also challenged by lack of resources, in terms of both staffing and equipment in the UK, but our vocation underpinned by values discussed in Chapter 2 keeps us motivated and well.

Learning points

1. Trust can be understood as the promise of a good future relationship, all things being equal.
2. Trust in the classroom is also about relationships and is the opposite of ruling by fear.
3. Trust has a relationship to behaviours such as fairness, caring, reliability, predictability, continuity and honesty or authenticity, which are just a few qualities that good teachers need.
4. Building trust is important, and it is about finding a balanced relationship. The teacher is not a friend or a parent but may have some of the positive qualities of these relationships.
5. Thinking about safeguarding the child, we also need to think about safeguarding ourselves and developing resilience.
6. A trust-based school culture embraces:
   - The ability to speak openly;
   - The ability to be adult;
   - The ability to see failure as an opportunity to learn;
   - The ability to give and receive robust, curious feedback (Davies, 2021, p. 36);
7. A trust-based culture leads to outcomes of collaboration, upskilling one another, improved teaching and wellbeing.

Challenge questions

1. Who do you trust and why?
2. Who do you distrust and why?
3. How resilient are you, thinking about the Grotberg model?
4. How would you manage your own resilience, if you feel you are not very resilient?
5. What external supports do you already have?
6. What would you say are your own personal strengths?

References

Adams, C., & Forsyth, P. (2009). The nature and function of trust in schools. *Journal of School Leadership* 19, 126-153.

Bruney, G. (2012). *The teacher-student relationship: The importance of developing trust and fostering emotional intelligence in the classroom*, a research paper submitted in conformity with the requirements for the degree of Master of Teaching Department of Curriculum, Teaching and Learning. Ontario Institute for Studies in Education of the University of Toronto, Canada.

Bryk, A., & Schneider, B. (2002). *Trust in schools: A core resource for improvement*. Russell Sage Foundation, New York, US.

Centre for Courage & Renewal & Francis, S.L. (2018). *The courage way: Leading and living with integrity*. Berrett-Koehler Publishers, Oakland, CA.

Davies, J. (2021). *The trust revolution in schools: How to create performance and collaborative culture*. Routledge, Abingdon, OX.

Forsyth, P., Barnes, L. & Adams, C. (2005). *Trust-effectiveness patterns in schools*. https://www.emeraldinsight.com/0957-8234.htm

Grotberg, E. (1995). A guide to promoting resilience in children: Strengthening the human spirit. *Early Childhood Development: Practice and Reflections No. 8*. The International Resilience Project, Bernard van Leer Foundation, the Netherlands.

Hattie, J. (2023). *Visible learning: The sequel*. Routledge, London.

Kay, J. (2017). Kinder, In *Ten poems of kindness*. Candlestick Press, Nottingham, UK.

Reich, J., Zautra, A., & Hall, J.S. (2010). *Handbook of adult resilience*. The Guilford Press, New York, NY.

5 Kindness

> There are good reasons for understanding kindness to be a natural predisposition. In fact, the word 'kind' has the same etymological roots as 'kin', 'kindred,' (family) and 'kind' (type). This is suggestive of a natural relationship of kindness between members of the same family, group or species.
>
> (Rowland, 2009, p. 207)

Introduction

Clegg and Rowland (2010) describe how students readily see kindness as a mark of the good teacher. Yet the concept of kindness is singularly silent in accounts of teaching excellence and student satisfaction, with only a minor place in professional values. It seems to have little place in a world, Clegg and Rowland argue, that is driven by competitive individualism. The academic literature on kindness favours thinking about how to teach children to be kind and focuses on kindness, or the lack of it, in university pedagogy. We can probably all remember or know teachers who are kind and accordingly helped us most to learn.

Performativity

Rowland (2009) explains that, from an educational perspective, and drawing on Lyotard's 'report on knowledge' with its concept of the 'terrors of performativity' (1984), Stephen Ball has analysed how a culture of tests, performance indicators, surveillance and audit have led practitioners to 'find their values challenged or displaced by the terrors of performativity' (Ball, 2003, p. 216). Ball describes performativity as a technology, a culture and a mode of regulation that employs judgements, comparisons and displays as means of incentive, control, attrition and change based on rewards and sanctions. The performances of individuals or organisations serve as measures of productivity, output or displays of 'quality'. As such they stand for the worth, quality or value of an individual or organisation within a field of judgement.

The teacher, researcher or academic, Ball explains, are subject to a myriad of these judgements, measures, comparisons and targets. Information is collected continuously, recorded and published, often in forms such as league tables, and performance is also monitored by activities such as peer reviews, site visits and inspections. There is a high degree of uncertainty and instability, which can cause anxiety; a sense of being constantly judged in different ways, by different means, according to different criteria, through different agents and agencies. There is a flow of changing demands, expectations and indicators that makes one continually accountable and constantly recorded (Ball, 2003).

There are other 'costs,' Ball further explains. A kind of values schizophrenia may be experienced by individual teachers, where commitment, judgement and authenticity within practice may be sacrificed for giving a good impression and performance. Ball explains the consequences of this. Teachers are no longer encouraged to have a rationale for practice or account for themselves in terms of a relationship to the meaningfulness of what they do but instead are required to produce measurable and 'improving' outputs and performance. Performance has no room for caring.

Kindness, Rowland argues, is one such displaced value. He adds a love of knowledge and a concern for social justice are other values lost. A consultation of a thesaurus provides us with synonyms for kindness. These are all slightly old-fashioned words: tenderness, compassion, sympathy, charity, generosity, humanity, benevolence. We cannot help wondering why they sound old-fashioned. All of them have in common caring for others and taking account of others' needs rather than looking out for self.

'Kindness' is arguably found to be 'out of place' in talk about education (Rowland, 2009). It can be seen as suggesting a feminine and, unfortunately in our society, a lower status approach – a sentimental and unrigorous or not stiff approach – and is accordingly, in some circles, valued lower than achievement of performativity measures. Language may be seen as something which constitutes or shapes the social world rather than being a reflection of the pre-existing social world. 'Discourse' is a term used to describe a set of ideas that go together and that interpret our experiences; they affect the way we think and talk about our experience and the way that we respond to it (Ryan, 2001). Discourses of kindness and caring are currently excluded or marginalised, we suggest, from discourse about what is good teaching at a policy and political level in some countries. With evidence-based learning, standards and performance indicators, the 'harder' discourse has overtaken the 'softer' virtues. Alison describes some of the softer old-fashioned virtues in the following section.

The importance of *savoir-être*, or knowing how to be

> I've been lucky.
>
> I was raised with kindness and caring by two parents, whose prime aim was for their children to be honest, mindful of others before self, humble, non-judgemental and to be happy and kind.
>
> I was lucky to have kind, caring and nurturing primary school teachers, male and female, who reassured us that we were cared *for* and *about* and that our learning was contingent on mutual respect, mutual endeavour, successes and failures, from which we would learn.
>
> I was lucky to have some very kind secondary school teachers. But I was unlucky to have some very unkind teachers, who belittled pupils when we found learning difficult, when we lacked artistic skills, when we couldn't climb the ropes in the gym hall or when we failed important, life-altering examinations.

When I worked with prospective bachelor of education (BEd) students, I was immediately struck by how many of them were frightened of 'academic' writing, as I was myself. A failed Higher Qualification in English in my senior fifth year and the feelings of inadequacy and the fear of writing stayed with me throughout my career. For the BEd students, assignments were such an important part of their beginning teacher life but were frequently perceived by them as unnecessary, a burden and a daunting challenge, when all they wanted to do was to be in the classroom with children and 'teach.' Kindness in that context meant caring for them, wanting good things for them and striving to understand their feelings and the emotional whirlwind that writing threw them into.

So, we had extra non-tutorial sessions, one-to-one chats, opportunities for them to let me hear them think. And so often, these opportunities were all that was needed. They simply didn't want to feel or be seen as 'stupid'!

And then, I started my master of research (MRes) programme in the last two years of my 40-year teaching career. You will not be surprised to read that having to write assignments and write a dissertation occasioned the resurgence of all these skilfully hidden feelings of inadequacy.

I was lucky again.

Karen McArdle was our tutor in year two and was also the supervisor for my dissertation. We would have regular catch-up meetings, and I remember vividly steeling myself outside her office door, with a draft paragraph or two for her to read and comment upon. I felt like a recalcitrant 17-year old. Karen was not responsible for me feeling like this, but her savoir-être, her way of being, literally changed my sense of self.

She listened, actively and non-judgementally; she smiled and nodded her head; she thought alongside me; all the subtle messages she conveyed reassured me that I was 'worthwhile, okay, getting there' (my words, never hers!). I heard the authenticity in her voice, the caring for a fellow human being struggling to overcome anxieties and fears. She saw things from my perspective and encouraged me every step of the way. She had high expectations for me and for the other members of our small group, but every word was underpinned by kindness. I felt joy and a sense of wonder on completion of my dissertation. She had brought me so much because she lived her values.

To quote in French again, she made me feel *bien dans ma peau* – at ease with myself – a gift for any teacher to give their pupil.

The systems and structure of the harder discourse stem from the culture of modernity or mass production, where quality systems were about quantity and standards and performativity was about throughput and measurable performance indicators. These indicators, arguably, may have a place but appear to have become an either/or binary necessity rather than being a both-and, which includes the softer values and virtues.

Why kindness matters

Ferguson (2017) argues in a community context that kindness matters for reducing social isolation, tackling loneliness and improving wellbeing, as well as providing the 'building blocks for community empowerment through positive relationships and values' (p. 3) Ferguson also indicates other factors that affect cultures of kindness. She is thinking about communities, but schools are a community, residing in a community, and so this is relevant to professional practice.

The first factor that Ferguson describes affecting cultures of kindness is levels of inequality. 'Poverty and disadvantage impact on our ability to form and maintain relationships' (p. 3). History and culture is a second factor affecting cultures of kindness. 'Places have their own distinctive stories that impact on their culture of kindness' (p. 3). The third factor that affects a culture of kindness is individual experiences: 'Individual biographies, mental health and resilience impact on our community relationships' (p. 3). Accordingly, there can be cultures where we work that impede kindness. You might like to consider your own work context and how it facilitates or militates against kindness.

The connection between kindness and teaching rests on the fact that both kindly acts and pedagogical acts require the actor to identify with the concerns of the other person. In serving the needs of the child, the good teacher attempts to see things from the child's perspective (Rowland, 2009). How teachers, leaders, parents and students *think* matters most.

> Their mind frames, ways of thinking, interpreting and evaluating, are core to the success of teaching. It is their thinking that leads to their choice of interventions, deciding and explaining their learning intentions and success criteria, knowing when a student is successful in attaining those intentions or not, having sufficient understanding of the students' understanding that they bring to the task and knowing sufficient about the content to provide meaningful and challenging experiences in various progressive pathways to success in learning.
>
> (Hattie, 2023, p. 7)

Some things can get in the way of kindness, according to Ferguson (2017). First, she describes the feeling of personal risk when we interact with others. Will the class or a child get out of control? Will they play up if I am too lenient? A difficulty with kindness is its confusion with leniency. In wanting a kind teacher, does the student really want one who will be lenient, soft and prepared to overlook errors and shallowness of thought? asks Rowland (2009). In wanting to be kind, is the teacher really motivated by the learner's needs or simply avoiding responsibility for the learner's confrontation with the inevitable pain of learning?

A second barrier to kindness that Ferguson (2017) proposes is regulation. Systems and structures for risk management in human interaction can get in the way of kindness. Professionalism or a dominant model of the dispassionate professional may impact on one's ability to see kindness as appropriate behaviour. Finally, Ferguson suggests performance management can fall short of measuring what matters. Narrow performance indicators, as described earlier, can push us away from focusing on our values.

Karen remembers a headteacher of a primary school who appeared to be a stereotypical consummate professional. She was always perfectly dressed, not a hair out of place; her office was tidy and minimalist. She carried a smart briefcase. When I first met her, I was a little intimidated, but she put me at ease at our first meeting when she opened her briefcase and showed me what was inside. She produced a packet of cornflakes and a litre of milk to provide breakfast for the children who would otherwise be hungry. This was before breakfast clubs became a common feature in schools. Kindness led her to take it upon herself to find a solution to a problem, hunger, for some children.

A child in Penny's class said this:

> What would you like him or her to be like?
> A kind teacher who would explain something in a
> easy way and would be kind and caring.

Figure 5.1 A child in Penny's class said this

Figure 5.1 shows what a child in Penny's class said. He/she knew exactly what would help her learn and had their very own understanding of the words 'kind' and 'caring.'

Kindness and professional values

Encouragingly, kindness appears in the 2019 professional standards of the Scottish General Teaching Council. Under the professional value of 'integrity,' teachers are expected to 'Demonstrate kindness, honesty, courage, and wisdom' (GTCS Standards, 2021).

These values were written following a review in 2012 by the GTCS, who commissioned the charity Children in Scotland to engage directly with children specifically around values and what mattered to children. The key finding was: Teachers should be kind and fair, meeting the needs of all pupils as individuals using a relationship-based and rights-based approach (Children in Scotland, 2018;).

In line with the Get It Right for Every Child (GIRFEC) agenda, Scottish education has a clear focus on wellbeing and relationship-based approaches to support children and young people, which is influenced by the UN Convention on the Rights of the Child (UNCRC). It promotes a range of resources, including:

- Applying nurture, whole-school approach to nurture approaches;
- Compassionate and connected classrooms;
- Respect for all.

Many of these resources are aimed at supporting both the teacher and pupils to build a culture of empathy and kindness in the school.

In England, while there are no references to kindness in the professional teaching standards, schools are now inspected on the personal development of pupils. Reassuringly, there are numerous examples of schools praised for developing a culture of kindness. This reinforces the importance of kindness at all levels and not just something to be taught as a discrete lesson to pupils.

Classroom management and the role of kindness

Classroom management is a hotly contested issue and is a challenge for many teachers, particularly newly qualified teachers. John remembers the early years of his teaching career, times struggling to 'control' the classroom and feeling embarrassed when a member of the senior management team had to step in. John remembers being told, 'Don't smile until Christmas.' The message being, before you can be Miss Honey, the kind-natured teacher from Roald Dahl's *Matilda*, you need to be a little bit of the terrifying Miss Trunchbull. Fortunately, over the years, John recognised this advice to be misguided.

There are plenty of books and guidance on classroom management, but interestingly three examples that have had a major influence on schools across the UK share a similar message: Establish clear routines within a culture of kindness and respect.

In 2001, Sue Crowley's popular and influential book *Get the Buggers to Behave* (2001) argued that by setting clear, positive expectations and building a supportive classroom culture, teachers can create a framework within which students are more likely to display positive behaviour. The book asked teachers to reflect on the root of the behaviour, the need for consistent routines, fair reward systems and the importance of positive relationships built on teachers embodying patience, fairness and respect.

In the mid 2000s, Jenny Mosley had a huge influence with her book *Better Behaviour through Golden Time* (2005). Children up and down the country followed the golden rules and enjoyed Golden Time. One of the golden rules was, 'We will be kind and helpful.' Schools were encouraged to explore these rules through circle time to ensure consistency in their application, and staff were expected to actively demonstrate positive behaviours and expectations to pupils.

Later on, Paul Dix published *When Adults Change, Everything Changes* (2017), arguing for visible consistency and visible kindness. He suggested we need to be rigorously consistent with routines and expectations but within a culture of kindness. Kindness means showing an interest in the pupils, having high expectations and trying to understand where the behaviour comes from and working together, restoratively, to make improvements (See Chapter 8: Tolerance and patience).

The importance of kindness by ensuring fairness, high expectations and going the extra mile is highlighted in Katriona O'Sullivan's (2023) autobiography *Poor*. In the book, she shares a story of one teacher's kindness that had a profound effect on her life. From the start of school, Katriona was being called names for smelling of urine. One day she was quietly asked to go the bathroom by her teacher Miss Arkinson. In there was the teaching assistant, Miss Hall, and a plastic bag.

> Miss Hall crouched down and said, quietly and kindly, 'Katriona, you're not in trouble, we are going to help.'
>
> (p. 29)

In the bag were clean knickers, a towel and soap and she was taught how to wash and told a fresh bag will be there every day.

> I stood there in clean pants with clean legs.
> 'Now' she said, 'what a great girl.'
> I felt as though I was standing in a beam of sunlight. She will never know what she did for me, how in that small bundle of towel, flannel and pants, Miss Hall gave me power. In that small bathroom every morning, before the other girls came in, I was in control of one thing.
>
> (p. 31)

The kind teacher

So, what is a kind teacher? We believe a kind teacher is cognisant of the joy and wonder that can characterise childhood. She or he can and does see the world from the child's perspective. The kind teacher cares for the children and about them, seeing and recognising their feelings. The kind teacher has consideration for others, generosity and provides humble help (see Chapter 7 on Humility and empowerment). Kindness, we suggest, is learnt through experience and cannot be faked. Children can spot inauthenticity from a mile off. Kindness enables socialising and promotes confidence and self-esteem. We can model 'please' and 'thank you' and greeting everyone. Smiling at children may be the only smile they get that day. Noticing is important, especially noticing the children who think they are not important enough to be noticed.

Kindness is linked to reassurance that making mistakes is okay. Listening attentively, nodding and smiling are all important even if they do not seem so. Making small moments of celebration is a kind thing to do, such as milestones or birthdays. All the authors are aware of moments of kindness in school that they will never forget. Kindness is memorable. If you ask adults about the teacher they most admired at school, it will not be the cleverest; it will often be the kindest.

Following are a number of quotes from Penny's school when asked, 'What makes a good teacher?'

> What makes a good teacher?
> A teacher that teaches well, is kind and funny to her/his students.
> A teacher that understands that not everyone has the same learning ability.
>
> What makes a good teacher?
> A teacher that has kindness but also some discipline.
> The teacher should care aout the students but also shouldn't have any favourites and be loving.
>
> What makes a good teacher?
> Good education, some strictness and kindness.

Figure 5.2 Quotes: "What makes a good teacher?"

Figure 5.2 shows a number of quotations from children at Penny's school about what makes a good teacher.

Learning points

- Performativity, the act of chasing outcomes and improvement targets, runs the risk of displacing important values like kindness.
- Kindness is important for improving social isolation, increasing wellbeing and empowering pupils.
- Cultures of kindness can be affected by levels of inequality, an organisation's history and individual experiences.
- Kindness means thinking about the child from their point of few, which is also the key to successful pedagogy.
- Classroom management should be rooted in a culture of kindness at all levels across a school community.

Challenge questions

1. Do you believe that kindness is important? Please justify your answer.
2. How could you contribute to a culture of kindness? What are your motivations?
3. Have you had an experience where you have seen concerning behaviour from the child's perspective? What difference did it make if you did? If not, what do you need to do to see things from a child's perspective?
4. Can you think of a time when you showed a child you noticed them and felt compelled to go the extra mile to providing care and reassurance? How did this feel for all parties?

References

Ball, S.J. (2003). The teacher's soul and the terrors of performativity. *Journal of Education Policy* 18(2), 215-228.
Children in Scotland. (2018). GTCS report. GTCS. https://childreninscotland.org.uk/wp-content/uploads/2022/01/Children-In-Scotland-Review-of-Professional-Standards.pdf
Clegg, S., & Rowland, S. (2010). Kindness in pedagogical practice and academic life. *British Journal of Sociology of Education* 31(6), 719-735.
Crowley, S. (2001). *Get the buggers to behave*. Continuum International Publishing Group.
Dix, P. (2017, 29 June). *When the adults change, everything changes*. Independent Thinking Press.
Ferguson, Z. (2017). *The place of kindness: Combating loneliness and building stronger communities*. Carnegie UK Trust.
GTCS Scotland. (2021). *The standard for full registration*.
Hattie, J. (2023). *Visible learning: The sequel*. Routledge, Abingdon, UK.
Mosely, J. (2005). *Better behaviour through golden time*. LDA.
O'Sullivan, K. (2023.) *Poor*. Sandycove.
Rowland, S. (2009). Kindness, *London Review of Education*, 7(3), 207-210.
Ryan, A. (2001). *Feminist ways of knowing: Towards theorising the person for radical adult education*. NIACE, Leicester, UK.

6 Courage

Introduction

> A brave person is not one who does not fear but is one who conquers fear. – Attributed to Nelson Mandela
>
> The Courage to Teach builds on a simple premise; good teaching cannot be reduced to technique, but is rooted in the identity and integrity of the teacher. Good teaching takes myriad forms, but good teachers share one trait: they are authentically present in the classroom, deeply connected with their students and their subject. These connections are held in the teacher's heart – the place where intellect, emotion, and spirit converge in the human self. Good teachers weave a life-giving web between themselves, their subjects and their students, helping their students learn how to weave a web for themselves.

The preceding quotation paragraph is taken from the dustjacket of a book called the *Courage to Teach* (2017, Twentieth Anniversary Edition) by Parker J. Palmer. The quotation is a collection of sentiments that we share. Palmer goes on to say that, 'every profession that attracts people for "reasons of the heart" is a profession in which people and the work they do suffer from losing heart' (2017, p. xxii). Relational trust, discussed in the previous chapter, helps with this and is important too for courage. Palmer defines relational trust as empathy, commitment, compassion, patience and the capacity to forgive.

Courage may be defined as a quality of mind that enables a person to face possibly negative consequences, such as difficulty, embarrassment, shame, pain or danger. It is a term first recorded in Middle English (1250-1300) and is derived from Latin, via Old French meaning heart. 'Heart' in its ancient meaning is the place where intellect, emotion and spirit converge (Palmer, 2017). Words related to courage are many, and we choose to include daring, persistence, tenacity, determination, endurance, fortitude, firmness, spirit, valour and adventurousness, all of which are different but capture what we might do in our teaching.

Courage often, in our view, represents overcoming vulnerability. Courage is not having no fear; rather it is overcoming fear, as indicated in the quotation from Nelson Mandela at the beginning of the chapter. It may be seen as a bridge between the values we hold and the sometimes-difficult enactment of those values. It is also about taking a risk – a risk of those consequences mentioned earlier of shame, embarrassment and pain and, of course, of being wrong. Recognising one's own mistakes requires courage since it may jeopardise authority, but we consider this to be very important and part of the integrity and authenticity of teaching. The rewards might be thought of as achievement, value consistency, self-esteem and the sheer delight in doing something that is right and works, particularly for other people. Penny describes her own experience doing something that caused her anxiety, teaching algebra, but which was right and worked.

Courage in teaching algebra to primary pupils

Algebra was introduced into the year 6 maths English curriculum a few years ago.

Initially, I was concerned about teaching this subject as I had never really understood algebraic equations at secondary school. However, it was essential to set a good example to the pupils, so I made sure my subject knowledge was secure. I was then able to teach all of the algebra materials methodically and carefully, paying special attention to those children who misunderstood key points. At the end of our series of lessons, I discussed with them how I hadn't understood algebra at school. They were really surprised and pleased. One of the children said it was really good I'd said this, because it made them feel more comfortable, and many of them thought it was teaching them a good example of resilience, in a different way from climbing a mountain.

Courageous acts need to be embedded in reflection. In particular, ask yourself *why* you are undertaking a courageous act. The adage, 'Teach the class you've got, not the one you want' – is important. There is a fine line between being brave and being wrong, we suggest. Yes, keep your eyes and ears open for new things to avoid being set in your ways, but exercise a balanced judgement in the likely efficacy and impact on the children and colleagues of any action.

Underpinning appropriate courageous behaviour is knowing one's craft. This is knowing when to be courageous and when to think outside the box, knowing when things are not working or when you are losing control and knowing when to stop. Knowing one's craft comes with reflection, time and experience.

We also need a moral compass in courageous acts. For example, we need to avoid making all children think the same way we do about any topic. We need to be sensitive to the family and community by not being extreme or radicalising children. Children do not live in a vacuum. Courage can be misguided, of course. You need to be aware of the social environment for the children. The authors can remember times when being gay was never mentioned in schools and would have been controversial, and now, of course, it is rightly commonplace.

Courage for the child

Engendering courage in the child is a wonderful thing to do. For some children, just coming to school demands courage. We do not necessarily know what the child has to overcome to get to school. The courage they show may be linked to their trust that they will not be belittled in any way, and this is in the teacher's control. So, we, as teachers, need to recognise and respect courage, which might also be linked to trying out our new courageous ideas. It is helpful to think of courageous acts as being red, amber or green for the child. Amber is a positive challenge or a stretch for the child, green is an easy ask by the teacher and red is a risky challenge for the child. We suggest sticking mostly to amber with creative ideas.

Courage in the organisation

The significance of courage in organisations is related to its contagious effect. Acts of courage may be felt far beyond the original incident, since they involve strong emotions that become widely shared via interpersonal exchanges and organisational stories and culture (Dor-Haim & Nir, 2023). We tend to think of moral courage in relation to teaching, but Dor-Haim and Nir (2023) describe social courage as an intended behaviour in which individuals may undermine and risk the esteem they obtain from others. Psychological courage involves the willingness to act, while facing the loss of psychological stability and experiencing irrational fears and anxieties.

Discussing the role of school leaders, Dor-Haim and Nir cite (2023) school principals' acts of courage as being defined by their willingness to resolve a complicated situation, acknowledge mistakes and learn from a given situation (Eisenschmidt et al., 2019). This includes the willingness to step out of their own comfort zone, accept criticism and promote change within themselves if required, as courageous acts. We suggest that this would apply to teaching staff too as we all strive to be leaders. Additionally, Dor-Haim and Nir discuss how studies that have examined school principals' courage have highlighted the humanistic and ethical aspects of their behaviour.

Sandra is an executive headteacher at a two-form entry primary school and a separate nursery school in Rochdale, England. She has been a headteacher for 24 years. She describes the courage she had to introduce outdoor learning in her school, in conversation with Penny.

Sandra: Although I have loved being a teacher and previously a deputy headteacher, I absolutely love being a headteacher as it has given me the opportunity to put things in place that will make a lasting difference to many children's lives in Rochdale, hopefully affecting the lives of future generations.

My two schools are in highly vulnerable and deprived areas of Rochdale, and many children enter the schools with very limited experiences. Most children had travelled no further than the end of their own street, and the typical day for each child included going to school, going to mosque and going home for tea. Although the school delivered all aspects of the curriculum, this was not an experiential curriculum, and the day-to-day learning of the children was far from memorable.

Penny: What inspired you to introduce outdoor learning?

Sandra: I am an active and adventurous person in my own personal life and have always encouraged my own children and my friends to lead the same life. Travelling to different countries and places in the UK in our campervan, engaging in adventurous pursuits including water sports, climbing and walking was part of our weekly leisure time. At the end of each day, it was very obvious that everybody who was part of these activities laughed, chatted and joked about the funny things that had happened during the day – widening the vocabulary, confidence and ambition of my children and their friends.

Many of the families at my schools did not have the opportunity to experience any of the things that my family did, so I wanted to change this. I wanted to ensure that all children were able to experience the opportunities that 'rich children' experience, and being in the position of the headteacher at the schools allowed me to do this.

At each school, the design of the curriculum-led adventurous pursuits programme, delivered by our outdoor team started slowly, accelerating into a wide range of first-hand experiences. Outdoor learning experiences are delivered every day across the whole school by the three full-time members of the outdoor team.

All children now have a progressive programme from reception to year 6 (age 11) of the following adventurous pursuits:

- **Cycling:** Balance bikes and age-appropriate sets of bikes;
- **Climbing:** Mobile small climbing wall in school, local climbing walls in Rochdale, larger climbing walls in the city and outdoor crag climbing in year 5;
- **Watersports:** Including mini-splash/inflatables in reception at a local lake, rafted canoes in nursery, reception and year 1 (age 6), sit on top canoes in year 2 (age 7) upwards, kayaks in year 3 (age 8) upwards and sailing in year 4 (age 9) upwards;
- **Horse riding:** Every Friday with children from year 3 (age 8) upwards. This is focused on the needs of special educational needs (SEN) children as well as identified children that we consider would benefit;
- **Archery:** In all year groups progressing from foam and suckers to pointed arrows;
- **Forest school:** Across the whole school using the two onsite dens and fire circles, delivered by an in-house forest school teacher; children learn to whittle wood, create structures, build teams, light fires and cook outside in addition to blow away art and forest art;
- **Residentials:** Residential stays are something that we encourage across most year groups to develop the children's confidence, independence, survival skills, team building and experiences. Children attend a residential that includes staying away from home from year 3. All residentials are offered at a very low cost, and we ensure that all children are supported to have the financial capacity to attend;
- **Transport:** The school owns two fully equipped minibuses and a transport van that are used to transport to any of the above;
- **Charging:** The school does not ask for any voluntary contributions to our day-to-day visits but does ask for a voluntary contribution towards the heavily subsidised residential visits.

Penny: How important is it for children to have the chance to experience residential learning?

Sandra: The opportunity to attend an affordable residential is a very important part of our outdoor learning offer. In our view, this adds to the soft skills that all children

should develop through primary schools and beyond, including team work, confidence, bravery, independence, problem solving, friendship bonds, an appreciation of nature and a healthy separation from parents.
We feel that this prepares children for adult life!
The school ensures that all parents can fund the small voluntary contribution to all aspects of outdoor learning including residentials, but to subsidise this heavily, the school earmarks a significant chunk of the school budget to pay for accommodation, staff, equipment and resources. The senior leadership team are committed to ensuring that every child has the opportunity to participate in all outdoor learning that is on offer.

The reputation of the school and the strong offer of a consistent approach to outdoor learning attracts many parents to enrol their children at the school, which in turn increases the budget of the school. This creates a win-win situation for the school, the children and the parents.

Penny: Would you advocate all schools have similar strategies for all round education?

Sandra: I am passionate about the benefits of outdoor learning and would advocate this approach to all schools. However, financial constraints, staff training, confidence, risk aversion and fear can create barriers to making the decision to take the plunge. I am incredibly lucky that the staff and governors at my school are 100% committed to the outdoor learning programmes that we have in place and can see the massive benefits to all children.

I feel that taking the plunge at my schools was the one of the best decisions of my career!

Alison describes one of her own courageous moments in the following section, when she was faced with a situation that contradicted her idea of what was right for the learners.

Hands off our pupils!

It is sadly often still the case that children with additional learning needs are withdrawn from modern languages classes because of conventional opinions about the so-called limits of the child.

- 'They don't need a modern language. They'll never use it.'
- 'They have difficulty in learning English, let alone another language.'
- 'Only learning support teachers have the knowledge and skills to support them!'

Now there could be a variety of reasons behind this choice to exclude. Perhaps modern languages teachers don't want these children in their class because of a limited understanding of what differentiation entails. Perhaps headteachers may not want the exam pass rate to be lowered because of the children's inclusion in subjects that some find difficult to master. Interestingly, these children, in my experience, were never withdrawn from history, geography, the sciences, and maths. I saw no reason to have them withdrawn from our classes!

But I had to fight for it, and not only with the headteacher or the support for learning teacher, but also with some members of my own department. It took time to convince them that we were responsible for the learning of *every* child in our classes – to convince them to trust each other – and it took courage as well to withstand the relentless challenge from colleagues in the staffroom and from the headteacher.

On many occasions, I felt vulnerable and frightened in case my stance would hurt the children I taught instead of supporting them. I wanted, however, to take a stance in defence of my principles of inclusion, even when others did not hold the same values.

I succeeded. My relationship with my learning support colleagues changed for the better. The department invited them to departmental meetings; we sought advice on presentation of resources. We invited these support colleagues into the classroom to learn with the children, and that had a strong influence on the very children who might have been withdrawn from the classes. We learned more about the subtleties of our craft and, indeed, not only 'talked the talk' of our values, but 'walked the walk' of them too. The courage paid off but had not been without risk.

Courage with the curriculum

The content of the curriculum will also have an effect on courageous acts. Curricula can sometimes be woolly or over-prescriptive, but it is important to have structure around what we, and others, choose to do in a classroom. You can be imaginative and push boundaries but need to be aware that some boundaries need to be maintained. We the authors think creativity is closely linked to courageous acts and thinking beyond usual boundaries can be very worthwhile where learning topics are challenging or potentially dull.

Risks are worth taking with our choices of how we teach and can be very effective. Following is a case study from a colleague, Ross McWhinnie, who was working in a difficult environment with people with additional support needs (ASNs). This case study shows what can be achieved with a creative imagination. Ross was working in a secondary school in Scotland. He was working with a group of eight ASN learners.

> I was made responsible for a group of learners undertaking a programme on Talking and Listening. There was a broad tapestry of barriers to learning that included autism, ADHD (attention deficit hyperactivity disorder) and Down's syndrome. The learners also came from different schools.
>
> A traditional approach to the unit would have been book study, with pupils listening to and responding to a text whilst building skills in line with their final assessment. On reflection, I felt that this was too passive an approach, potentially limiting of the imagination and unlikely to be stimulating to learners who have done this sort of activity all through their earlier school experience. Often the book selected was one that was written for younger readers and, whilst this could be a better fit for their reading age, it often seemed to me terribly unadventurous. To that end, while we did indeed pursue a book study, together we chose, rather surprisingly, Homer's *Odyssey*.
>
> Drawing on research into gamification techniques, I took the key events of the *Odyssey* and turned them into Dungeons and Dragons style adventures, played out on a wipe-clean roll mat. After a preamble, pupils were asked to make decisions on Odysseus' behalf based on what they had learned and felt about him, steering him through the Underworld or past Charybdis. As games-master, I guided events along the path of the

original story, but where pupils offered creative alternatives or made mistakes, these proved rich hinge-points for learning.

Before each lesson I developed question stems appropriate to each learner, so each had the opportunity to demonstrate their knowledge or opinion in a way appropriate to their needs. Responding to individual needs, some young people would only be required to make a simple choice to demonstrate improvement, whereas others would be expected to synthesise complex ideas.

I tracked the learners' progress by beginning each lesson with an extended recap designed as verbal retrieval practice, noting participation and retention, personal and staff observations, quiz scores, parental input and finally the outcomes of assessment. The pupils told me they loved this way of learning, and their ability to retell the *Odyssey* to their peers, complete with complex names, has been deeply heartening professionally. Next year they have already decided they would like to do *Beowulf*.

Parker J. Palmer, mentioned at the opening of this chapter, discusses the 'new professional' and the link to values, urging that we avoid passivity in the workplace. He calls for education for teachers for transformation, so that they can challenge and question all that they learn and do.

An education for transformation would raise up professionals in every field who have ethical autonomy and the courage to act on it, who possess knowledge and skill AND embody the highest values in their vocation.

(Palmer, 2017, p. 213)

Educators of teachers need to think about courage themselves and have courage to educate teachers to translate feelings into knowledge and action, so the teachers can question the establishment tenets of education productively and courageously. In this way teachers can question what is worng in an educational context.

Learning points

1. Educators should have courage, embrace their mistakes and then adjust and improve teaching methods over time.
2. We need to acknowledge mistakes, correct them when needed, and use them as teachable moments.
3. We should encourage courage in children, in different ways, both in and out of the classroom.
4. Standing up for students' needs against bureaucratic or systemic challenges takes bravery but is impressive.
5. We can aim to handle setbacks, failures, and difficult days with strength and perseverance.

Challenge questions

1. Can you think of a time when you have been courageous?
2. How did you feel?
3. Did you feel vulnerable?
4. What made you do something courageous, however small?
5. If you cannot think of a courageous act, can you think of a situation in learning and teaching that would make you courageous?
6. Can you think of a time when you were creative with the curriculum? What prompted this? How did you feel whilst making the change?

References

Dor-Haim, P., & Nir, A. (2023). Perceptions of courage: Elementary school leaders' perspectives. *Educational Management Administration & Leadership*). https://doi.org/10.1177/17411432231177534

Eisenschmidt, E., Kuusisto, E., Poom-Valickis, K., et al. (2019). Virtues that create purpose for ethical leadership: Exemplary principals from Estonia and Finland. *Journal of Beliefs and Values* 40(4), 433–446.

Palmer, P. J. (2017). *The courage to teach: Exploring the inner landscape of a teacher's life.* Jossey-Bass.

7 Humility and empowerment

Introduction

> The word 'humility' is derived from humus, a Latin word that means 'ground,' 'soil' or 'of the earth.' Humble persons are well grounded or rooted, inasmuch as their lives are centred in a healthy and liberating understanding of who they are. Humility frees people from having to pretend that they are more than, or other than, who they truly are. This suggests humility and genuine self-confidence are intimately connected.
>
> (Wadell, 2017, p. 53)

Humility is not about being humble or low; it is about focusing on others' needs as equals (Worthington, 2007). Humility, explains Worthington, is more than altruism, where the benefits are for self; humility is about seeing needs, feeling positive emotions towards others and acting to meet needs. Worthington suggests that to understand humility you can think of what we call unsung heroes, and what he calls the heroes of humility. What are the characteristics of the heroes that made you choose them? Perhaps your reflections will tell you what humility is about.

> It is not uncommon to associate humility with persons who exhibit a chronic lack of self-regard. They show an unhealthy submission to others, especially persons in authority, and an irritating inability to recognize, claim and use their gifts. But persons who have little regard for themselves, who continually see themselves as inferior to others and who don't speak up when they are mistreated, are not humble. They are failing to genuinely love and care for themselves.
>
> (Wadell, 2017, p. 53)

The preceding quotation discusses what humility is not. We suggest it is a complex notion and combines characteristics we have discussed in other chapters, especially trust, resilience and kindness. Next we list what we think humility brings to the classroom:

- Being prepared to admit mistakes and to learn from them;
- Showing empathy to colleagues and pupils;
- Listening to and hearing others;
- Being able to recognise one's own strengths and limitations;
- Knowing how to optimise strengths and manage limitations;

- Recognising where learning is required in skills, knowledge and abilities;
- Having a modest and well-judged opinion of oneself;
- Being able to self-reflect and self-respect;
- Being confident in one's own views and open to others' views;
- Being a good learner;
- Allowing oneself self-compassion;
- Being orientated to others.

Alison has a French phrase that summarises this list: *'bien dans sa peau,'* which we have used before in this book and which means being comfortable in your own skin, a quality that comes with time and experience. Humility brings you closer to the child and fosters an environment of trust and respect, an environment in which you as the teacher are really authentic and there for the child.

Humility, we suggest, is close to sympathy and compassion; it can be a single act or prolonged. We said earlier that it was not altruism, as that has benefits for the self, but so does humility in some ways. It can make you feel good. This is what Worthington calls an *'unsought by-product'* (p. 39). The motivation is not to feel good but to meet needs.

> True humility puts aside both narcissism and its entitlement sub-theme.
> (Worthington, 2007, p. 57)

It is important we do not see humility as being linked to low self-esteem. It involves modesty, self-knowledge and justified pride and confidence. It is interesting to note that some people choose the opposite of humility—almost arrogance—in their chosen leaders, particularly in politics at the time of writing, in our view.

You may be interested in the following advantages of humility cited *inter alia* by Ng (2012). She cites studies that found a link between humility and good academic performance by students. Although the cause of this correlation was unclear, it was consistent with proposals that humble individuals are open to novel ideas and have a strong desire to learn. Ng also cites literature that suggests that humble individuals adapt similarly well to life events, whether they involve mastering academic concepts, managing relationships or handling work challenges.

Humility is linked to relationships of power or mitigation of power and to meeting needs, and these we consider after Alison's story about humility.

The country mouse

On many occasions, I have observed the faces of those children who are struggling to understand what I am trying to teach: Their heads are lowered, not wanting to catch my eye in case I ask a question to which they do not know the answer; there is a discomfiture in their eyes; their facial expressions tell me so much—a frown, a nod of the head, that look of total incomprehension that we have all seen, I'm sure.

But if we want to empower the children, encourage confidence in them to tell us what they don't understand and to articulate their anxieties about the learning process, then we need to demonstrate our trustworthiness, our caring, our respect for the 'predicament' they find themselves in and our compassion and our willingness to share occasions when we too experienced these emotions. I told them the following true story.

Learning a foreign language is about more than learning a foreign language. It's about finding out who you are, how you feel about yourself as a foreign language speaker – or non-speaker. It's about daring and caring.

Up to the age of 14, I attended my local junior secondary school and was taught French and Latin by Mrs. Harley. My family lived in a council house, and we enjoyed summer holidays in a fisherman's cottage in Fife, Scotland. I was sent to France at the age of 12 to live with a family in Boulogne for a month. At that point, I was fluent in weather expressions, four irregular verbs and the numbers 1-100. Nothing more.

Catherine's family was bourgeois, owned a string of shoe shops and had a *résidence secondaire*, complete with a maid. They were rather bemused at this young, very naïve girl who had not been taught to use a knife and fork when eating a banana, who did not know that she had to use *vous* and not *tu* when talking to older people she did not know and who shied away from conversation because her vocabulary and knowledge of grammar did not allow her to engage in anything faintly resembling a conversation. I felt like the Country Mouse. I felt so inadequate.

But I stayed. My ability to understand and speak French grew exponentially – simply because it had to!

So I told the children that when I started to teach, I promised myself that I would never let any of my pupils feel that inadequacy, either in real life or in the classroom. If there was something they didn't understand, something they weren't enjoying, all they had to do was tell me – no judgement, no criticism. We would work together, side by side.

Needs

Speaking of needs to be met, people often refer to Maslow's hierarchy of needs, which is useful for categorising needs but is not useful as a hierarchy of needs. If you look at Figure 7.1, you will see that people cannot have certain spiritual or higher order needs without other basic needs being met and this just is not true of many religious populations in the world, who might suffer material discomfort but have highly developed religious views. As a tool for teaching, it can be useful in expressing how learning can fail to take place unless basic needs like hunger and comfort have been taken into account.

Meeting identified needs raises the issue of how needs are, indeed, identified, and we need to be aware that being 'needy' is seen as being cloyingly dependent in some quarters. So, we must be careful not to label people in this way. There are many ways of identifying needs of a class, group or individual child. This involves formal research and informal methods. In many cases it will be done through noticing or observing a child or children's behaviour, appearance and demeanour. We always need to be sure that we are careful and authentic in our interpretation of these.

Wadell (2017) describes in the healthcare profession how important humility is to meeting needs. You might like to think what this means for the teaching profession.

> One of the potential hindrances to excellence in health care is to gradually lose sight of patients as unique human beings with distinctive needs, fears and concerns. The more bureaucratized and depersonalized medicine becomes – and perhaps the more

Humility and empowerment 61

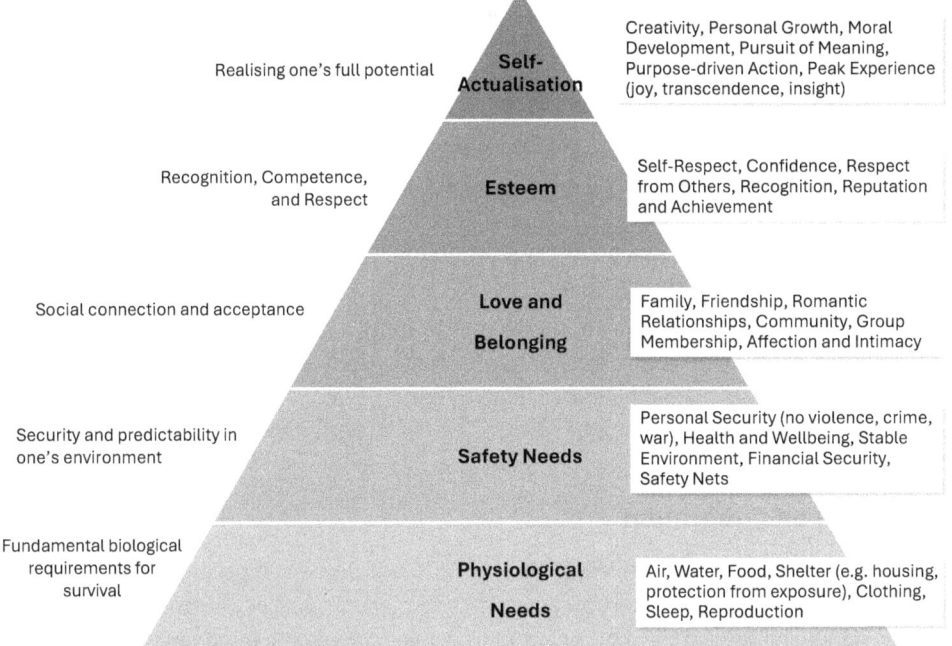

Figure 7.1 Maslow's hierarchy of needs

technical – the more likely it is that the personal dimension of medicine will be lost. A love informed by humility resists this depersonalization by reminding us that the relationship between health care providers and their patients is, from first to last, a human encounter in which a person in need comes for help.

(Wadell, 2017, p. 54)

Attunement

Talking about attunement leads to thinking about being on the same wavelength as the child. It is about meeting on an emotional level (Grimmer, 2024), and it includes empathising, using body language and tone of voice to indicate that we are really listening. Some of the ways to become attuned are described by Grimmer as follows:

- Responding sensitively to children in the moment;
- Fully focusing on the child;
- Closely observing and noticing their likes and dislikes;
- Being curious about what children are doing and why;
- Actively listening to children and acting upon this;
- Playing alongside children and co-constructing ideas.

(Derived from Grimmer, 2024, p. 19)

Belonging and welcoming children will assist with attunement. Children will feel at home where they are accepted and valued. This belonging will counter marginalisation and exclusion (Grimmer, 2024). Grimmer provides helpful ways of assisting children to feel they belong:

- Finding out details about them and building a relationship and secure attachment to them;
- Recognising comfort derived from 'snuggling in';
- Ensuring children see themselves and their families represented in the school setting;
- Offering the children a lot of opportunities to make decisions so that they feel part of the fabric of the classroom;
- Planning ahead for times of change to ensure that children feel safe and secure;
- Considering belonging needs and reflecting upon our welcoming learning environment, partnership with families and ethos.

(Derived from Grimmer, 2024, p. 20)

Power and empowerment

Power and humility are closely allied. Thompson (2007) explains how power is viewed with different orientations. He describes how power can be psychological or personal and embraces an individual's ability to achieve his or her aims. Power can also be discursive and cultural; it takes into account language and setting, such as in a doctor's surgery where the patient is less powerful than the doctor. Discourse is a bit more than language; it is about the interplay between language and people's relationships, in which some people are more powerful than others. Discourse becomes part of our culture and shapes assumptions and unwritten rules. A structural orientation refers to one's place in systems and structures of society, embracing access to resources and accordingly poverty and hunger; ideological assumptions about status and hierarchy, for example; and barriers to progress, such as the 'glass ceiling' for women's progress, says Thompson (p. 6). Power can also be understood as a person's disposition, such as authority or charisma, as Thompson explains.

Empowerment can be thought of as giving power to other people, but this is far too easy to say. Empowerment is more about working *with* children or adults to help them to gain greater control of their lives. Thinking back on Thompson's orientations to power, this means helping them to develop confidence, self-esteem and skills needed to further their goals. It also means they understand discrimination and can challenge stereotypes. Tackling structural limitations is less straightforward. 'Conscientisation' is a term used (Freire, 1996) to describe how adults can redress blame from self to structural inequalities, such as poverty not being their fault but the fault of society. With children we cannot hope to use conscientisation, but we can be aware of the views we are promulgating in the classroom about inequalities.

Grimmer (2024) explains how everyday routine can help children to feel competent by allowing them to make decisions and by following their lead in play. Grimmer provides a list of ways in which we can help children to feel empowered:

- Asking for children's views and opinions;
- Allowing children to make choices;

- Listening to them and acting on what they say;
- Including them in our conversations in age-appropriate ways;
- Playing alongside them, co-creating and co-constructing learning;
- Enabling through children by scaffolding task and activities;
- Supporting them to resolve conflicts;
- Teaching them strategies to use when adults are not present;
- Role modelling and offering works and phrases they can use, e.g., 'Can I play?'
- Promoting independence.

(Derived from Grimmer, 2024, p. 42)

Once again, thinking of healthcare professionals, Wadell (2017) describes how humility contributes to excellence:

> How, then, does humility contribute to excellence in health care? Humility makes for better health care professionals in many ways, but three seem most important: First, without humility, doctors and nurses – along with administrators, technicians, aides, social workers and pastoral care ministers– will not be sufficiently attuned to what always must be health care's central focus and abiding concern: the patient who is sick, frightened, vulnerable or confused. Humility helps everyone who attends to patients see them not as biological puzzles needing to be solved, but as unique persons in need of healing, care, understanding and compassion.
>
> (Wadell, 2017, p. 56)

Humility in different cultures

Humility is understood differently in different cultures. It is important to understand the conceptions of humility in the country in which you are working, or if you are working with recent migrant children, you need to be aware of the value placed on humility by parents and whether it is different for boys and girls. Harrison et al. (2023) undertook a study to investigate how teachers in Hong Kong conceptualize and enact humility in their practice. Their findings brought to light striking differences in the ways local and international schoolteachers assigned meaning to and introduced notions of humility into their work. The latter group saw both intellectual and cultural humility as central to their pedagogy and professional praxis, whereas the former group assigned a peripheral value to humility in their teaching, although they practiced humility in interactions with colleagues.

Harrison et al. (2023) describes how the influence of the neo-liberal discourse (discussed further in Chapter 12) places a great emphasis on traits and behaviours in teaching outcomes, such as extroversion, confidence, public performance and self-promotion, which seems at odds with the notion of humility.

Learning points

1. Humility is defined as having its origins in words meaning ground or earth. It is not about being humble or low; it is about focusing on another's needs without abusing any power we may have.

2. We refer to Maslow's hierarchy of needs and its insufficiency to explain needs as it does not always embrace spiritual needs.
3. Power and humility are closely linked and humility may be perceived differently by different cultures.
4. Humility brings *inter alia* to the classroom:

    a. Being prepared to admit mistakes to learn from them;
    b. Showing empathy to colleagues and pupils;
    c. Listening to and hearing others;
    d. Being able to recognise one's own strengths and limitations.

Challenge questions

1. Does humility seem old-fashioned to you? If so, why do you think this is the case?
2. Thinking of needs, can you see how the Maslow hierarchy works in practice for your teaching?
3. Empowerment is important for everyone, in our view. Do you agree? If so, how do you empower children?

References

Freire, P. (1996, original publication 1974). *The pedagogy of the oppressed*. Penguin Books, London.
Grimmer, T. (2024). *Loving pedagogy explained*. Routledge, London.
Harrison, M., Briffett-Aktaş, C., Ying, J., Tsui, G., Cheng, A.S., & Jackson, L. (2023). A comparative study of international and local school teachers' perceptions and enactments of humility in Hong Kong. *Beijing International Review of Education* 5(3), 217-241.
Maslow, A.H. (1943). A theory of human motivation. *Psychological Review*, 50(4), 370.
Ng, A. (2012). *Eating the humble pie: A non-defensive response to failures*. Thesis submitted for the degree of master of social sciences. Department of Psychology, National University of Singapore.
Thompson, N. (2007). *Power and empowerment*. Russell House Publishing, Lyme Regis, Dorset, UK.
Wadell, P. (2017). Humility: An indispensable virtue to learn for practising with excellence. *Health Progress*, 2017, 52-56.
Worthington, E. (2007). *Humility: The quiet virtue*. Templeton Foundation Press, Philadelphia, PA.

8 Tolerance and patience

While tolerance and patience seem similar, they possess attributes that differentiate them from one another. Tolerance implies there is something to tolerate that does not sit quite right with you. Patience can be about remaining composed in the face of frustration, understanding that things take time to unfold or resolve. We need to provide time, space and pacing for learning in the classroom. Tolerance is an inclusive behaviour about acceptance and empathy for children who might be challenging because of their behaviour or background. It also recognises diversity and acknowledges the idea that we all have our own perspectives and choices. In class, we are aware of the implications for many children during Ramadam, for example; some children may be more tired than others when family members are fasting - they will often eat before sunrise with family. This may or may not have an effect on their school day. They may also be hungry or tired. Tolerance often involves engaging with children to find common ground and to compromise about attitudes or behaviours. We need patience to be tolerant as we need to take a deep breath with some behaviours and be resilient. Patience is an emotional skill and assists us to be in control of what happens in the classroom. We need, of course, to attempt never to act impatiently with children. We need to be cognitively and emotionally patient, knowing our own limits. And this can be hard.

We also need, of course, to be tolerant of colleagues. Team teaching is increasingly common, and we need to be tolerant of other teachers' processes and learn to observe, reflect and learn from others' practice. We can step back and go with what happens when others are teaching and learn to observe, reflect and learn from others' practices.

Intolerance is important for some of our values. There are some aspects of the human condition, for example racism, exclusion and child protection issues, that we suggest demand intolerance.

Classroom management

Classroom management is the management of the place, students and sources. Preparing a suitable learning environment and creating and using the facilities and place, rules, learning programmes and processes are called classroom management (Bayraktar & Dogan, 2017). Classroom management is a complex structure that allows for the learning of students, ensures that they achieve identified learning objectives and consists of the behaviours used by teachers in order to explain and maintain classroom situations and that must be defined step by step. The main objective of discipline is to ensure that individuals are in harmony both with themselves and the environment by introducing them to certain habits, and to maintain the moral development of individuals with the sense of responsibility (Bayraktar & Dogan, 2017).

Initially, it is noted that notions of 'behaviour management' dominate discourses about school discipline. It is suggested that this is unhelpful, as behaviour management skills are underpinned by a behaviourist understanding of learning that denies pupils an important degree of agency over their own development. Pupils are rather portrayed as unruly or morally deficient or just bad (Bayraktar & Dogan, 2017).

Children may be disaffected at school for many reasons, for example, pace of teaching, boredom with lesson content, lack of engagement with the teacher and neurodivergence.

Palardy (1995) puts forward nine aspirational, we suggest, strategies for teachers for preventing discipline problems in the classroom:

1. They should be relaxed about themselves, their students and subject areas;
2. They should believe in the behaviours of their students regarding suitable classroom behaviours;
3. They should ensure interest in the learning activities;
4. They should combine the capacities of students with learning activities and requirements;
5. They should create the rules together with students;
6. They should ensure that students know and understand how the routine works;
7. Problem times should be determined;
8. They should not forget that students are not adults;
9. They should show that they actually respect students.

(Cited by Aydın, 2001, pp. 70-71)

Observing the behaviour of the children is the only evidence the teacher has about what pupils can do or will do and about what they believe. When children are often out of their seats, we may say they are hyperactive. That does not help to solve the problem. We must try to remember, however, that our interpretations are seen only through one lens. Such labels can be used as an excuse for doing nothing! Almost all classroom behaviour is learned:

- Learning involves changes in behaviour.
- Behaviour changes as a result of its consequences.

Behaviours are also influenced by classroom contexts.

(Sieberer-Nagler, 2016, p. 164)

In any situation, some behaviours are more appropriate than others. The teacher should look for a classroom organisation that is helpful to learning and teaching in a good way. When the young pupils have learned the new behaviour or behave as we want them to do regularly, then the teacher may maintain this behaviour more economically by reducing the frequency of reinforcement. Social reinforcement should always try to ensure that it is directed towards the behaviour rather than the person. The behaviour is inappropriate, not the child.

Teachers do sometimes ignore the internal obstacle, says Sieberer-Nagler (2016). They only look on the external problems. But when we have more control over the internal obstacles, we can often find better ways to cope with the external ones. Therefore, it is important to deepen your self-knowledge through introspective exercise. It is important to change counterproductive feelings and to look for positives, develop empathy and alter any restrictive goals. Every teacher can try to change her or his negative emotions into positive ones. You may see the glass half empty rather than half full. Negative attitudes are learned, and therefore they can be changed.

Children with demanding behaviours need patience and understanding. Classroom management is not about techniques or tricks; it is about understanding what is happening in the child's life and experience that causes unacceptable communication. See Alison's story in the following section.

Patience: It just takes time!

It was my first year of teaching many moons ago, when the first term lasted 18 weeks and continuing professional development was unheard of and undreamt of. Mentoring beginning teachers was unknown and deemed unnecessary. I was the sole teacher of French in a small junior secondary in Edinburgh, in an area that was called at that time an area of multiple deprivation.

I loved it. I was at home with these children, whose aspirations for the future were determined in many cases by the lives, past and present, of their parents. They were open, frank and spoke 'as they saw'! So, the lessons were either 'fab' or 'crap.' You learn quickly to assimilate their language because it's the basis of communication, isn't it?

Anyway, then there was James. He was an only child. His father worked offshore in the oil industry, and James was showered with presents whenever he came home. James was the envy of his classmates who couldn't aspire to the latest mobile, the latest XBox or the newest trainers. The envy and jealousy were palpable.

He was a bright boy but withdrawn and with a temper that could erupt in a matter of seconds. He scowled when he came into the classroom; scowled if I looked at him, hoping for an answer. He scowled when he left the classroom and muttered under his breath. In my arrogance and naivety, I thought that I would be able to transform this reluctant participant in my lessons – I could cajole him, bribe him with rewards, and then impatience and intolerance started to creep in, and at times I could feel knots of frustration and annoyance in my gut. It's so difficult at times to exercise self-control and restraint. But I did try.

Fast forward six months, and 52 children and four teachers were on a trip to Brittany. In the mornings, we would all go down to the beach and play French cricket, jump dunes, make sandcastles, play leapfrog, swim, picnic and talk – and James was finally transformed into the wee boy he so desperately wanted to be. He wanted to be allowed to be a child and to play childish games. No amount of the latest gadgets could make him as happy as he was on the beach. And all it took was patience: the belief and hope that over time he and I (and his classmates) could find a way of enjoying each other's company, in and out of the classroom. It opened up opportunities for him to resolve the issues that had been making him cross and withdrawn. And every now and again, he smiled in class. And that was perhaps the biggest 'wow' of all.

Children need to be calm to learn and not be frightened in class. They have to want to be there. Lesson plans can be dropped if behaviour demands this. Lesson plans are precisely that - plans - and plans need to be flexible, open to adjustments as the lesson develops; open to diversions and recapitulations if behaviours demand. But we need to read and interpret the behaviours. We have to teach the class in front of us, not the class we want. Classes are highly complex with perhaps autism and ADHD in the mix. This is a big challenge to the beginning teacher, but over time classroom management becomes easier. See Penny's story:

> We were going outside for break and some children started pushing, so I looked back, raised my eyebrows (apparently) and the pushing stopped. We arrived outside as the children started playing, when a group of girls came over, smiling broadly to say I was the best 'roaster.' Hadn't a clue what they meant, so they explained I manage to make them do things, without getting angry, but I make them think about what they are doing …. with my eyes. Thought this was hilarious - as did the children, when I didn't know the up-to-date term, 'roaster.'

Teachers cannot be perfect, but common sense is needed, such as not putting maths on the curriculum at 3.15 pm, near time to go home. Instead we can be asking, 'What effect is my teaching having on the children?' Patience is needed, so pacing yourself and pacing learning for the children are both important.

The structure and climate of classes set the scene for what happens in them.

> The desire is for the class to have social cohesion, great classroom management, minimal disruptive behaviour, high levels of friendship and no bullying, and appropriate interventions and counseling for those in need or more likely to affect other students.
>
> (Hattie, 2023, p. 182)

Behaviour

Paul Dix, teacher and teacher trainer, believes the foundation of every school must be excellent behaviour. However, he was frustrated with punitive behaviour management systems, which blamed and demoralised children and their families. He recognised the key to excellent behaviour was consistency. However, he warned against schools that had built a culture of 'restrictive consistency that limits flair and patronises poor communities,' which instilled 'the machismo of zero tolerance,' but instead he promoted a 'consistency routed in kindness,' which was 'palpable, audible and highly visible' (Dix, 2017, p. 3).

In his book, 'When the Adults Change Everything Changes', he wanted to show how 'small, persistent visible shifts in adult behaviour have an incredible effect on children's behaviour'. Through collaborative design the adults can create a 'this is what we do' ethos, where everyone, adults and pupils, are responsible for its success (2017, p. 6).

He shows how it requires an emotionally mature adult to react to situations with patience and certainty. Understanding 'how you behave is more important than how they behave.' He asks us to be 'bothered,' through 'daily acts of care, perpetual generosity of spirit and interest in their lives.' He challenges teachers to make restorative approaches our default mode rather than an endless cycle of detentions and time outs. To build positive relationships, to understand some children can often 'carry the invisible of traumatic lives' and become the 'predictable, consistent and empathetic adults' they need (2017, p. 141).

Classroom management, explains Hattie (2023), is a necessary but not sufficient condition for raising achievement. It typically involves establishing a positive climate, good relations among children and with the teacher, a sense of fairness and an invitation to learn. If classrooms are to be inviting places that are fair and safe, there is no place for bullying (Hattie, 2023). Bullying adversely affects the behaviour and learning of both bully and bullied; and intensive programmes were effective, says Hattie, including parental meetings, firm disciplinary methods and improved playground supervision. A whole-school policy works as long as it is augmented with other interventions. Poor behaviour needs fair, clear and understood consequences. Consequences matter.

A key factor in developing a positive classroom climate is classroom cohesion, the sense that all are working towards positive learning gains. Classroom cohesion, says Hattie (2023), includes goal directedness, positive interpersonal relations and social support. Hattie cites Haertel and Walberg (1980), who found that learning outcomes are positively associated with cohesiveness, satisfaction, task difficulty, formality and goal direction and negatively associated with friction, cliques, apathy and disorganisation.

A sense of belonging in the class is a powerful precursor to learning (Hattie, 2023, p. 205). Belonging refers to the extent that students feel personally accepted, respected, included and supported by others.

Learning points

1. We need patience to be tolerant, as we need to take a deep breath with some behaviours and be resilient.
2. Classroom management is the management of the place, students and sources – not behaviour management or 'discipline.'
3. Children can be disaffected at school for many reasons such as, for example, pace of teaching, boredom with lesson content or lack of engagement with the teacher.
4. Negative attitudes about children are learned, and therefore they can be changed.
5. We have to teach the class in front of us, not the class we want.

Challenge questions

1. Think of a time when you were impatient or cross with a pupil or pupils. Reflect on how you resolved this and how you might approach this in the future.
2. What aspects of the human condition are you intolerant of? How do these affect the way you interact with the children?
3. How do you create a secure and safe environment that vetoes bullying and aids learning and teaching?

References

Aydın, B. (2001). *İlköğretim okullarında sınıf disiplinin sağlanması*. Yayımlanmamış Doktora Tezi, Abant İzzet Baysal Üniversitesi Sosyal Bilimler EnstitÜsÜ, Bolu.

Bayraktar, H. V., & Dogan, M. C. (2017). Investigation of primary school teachers' perception of discipline types they use for classroom management. *Higher Education Studies*, 7(1), 30-45.

Dix, P. (2017). *When the adults change, everything changes: Seismic shifts in school behaviour*. Crown House Publishing.

Haertel, H., & Walberg, H. (1980). Investigating an educational productivity model. *Evaluation in Education* 4, 103-104.

Hattie, J. (2023). *Visible learning; the sequel*. Routledge, Abingdon, OX, UK.

Palardy, J. M. (1995). Dealing with misbehavior: Two approaches. Journal of Instructional Psychology, 22(2), 135.

Sieberer-Nagler, K. (2016). Effective classroom-management & positive teaching. *English Language Teaching* 9(1), 163-172.

PART THREE

In this section of the book, we consider the environment for teaching and teaching ideas. This includes nurturing, rights, wellbeing, knowledge, social justice and leadership, all of which have an impact on good teachers.

9 Things, place and time for children

One teacher told of the inconvenience, and even humiliation, of standing out in the hallway each morning, waiting amidst her students for the school principal to come by and unlock her classroom door.

(Fenwick & Edwards, 2010, p. 7)

Introduction

Thinking about the preceding quotation, we can see from Fenwick and Edwards (2010) that keys matter. They also describe the gym teacher who locked the gym to prevent accidents, whilst other teachers held gym activities in school hallways, jimmied the lock and retaliated by duplicating the key and locking the gym teacher out! Things and places matter to people, both adults and children. Karen remembers a professor of education recalling his childhood in primary school who felt overwhelmed by the size and noise of the classroom. His respite lay in the reading corner where books were stored and there was a screen, so he could find moments of what he described, as an adult, as solitude and peace. Places and spaces matter to children. Socialisation is important to many children, but to others solitude matters.

Things Matter

Fenwick and Edwards (2010) describe actor network theory (ANT), which assists with thinking how stuff or things matter. All things have associations and networks of correlated meaning.

> 'Playground', for example, represents a continuous collaboration of bats and balls, swing installations, fences, grassy hills, sand pits, children's bodies and their capacities, game discourses, supervisory gazes, safety rules and so on. This playground is both an assemblage or network of things that have become connected in a particular way, and an actor itself that can produce fears, policies, pedagogies, forms of play and resistance to them.
>
> (Fenwick & Edwards, 2010, p. 8)

Everyday things, Fenwick and Edwards (2010) explain, exert force and joining together, changing and being changed by each other. They form associations or networks that change and increasingly get bigger. They give the example of a maths textbook for children. It embeds a network of curriculum development; policy makers, computers, teachers and maths experts. Then there are the networks of publication: writers, editors, reviewers, drafts and printers.

DOI: 10.4324/9781032678283-12

There is then the network of distribution across school and classrooms locally or in a wider sphere. These networks can promote standardisation across space and time, and we need to consider if this is desirable.

Pedagogy, Fenwick and Edwards explain, is mediated by 'things.' Chalk, textbooks and desks are examples of things that can draw teachers together in a distinct network of materials, which can reaffirm practice and values for teachers working or in conversation together. Do they get taken for granted? Again, we need to think about them and their associations or networks. Things also accrue meaning from the past. They circulate in the midst of connection, cultural histories and symbolic values (Fenwick & Edwards, 2010), but they also compel certain forms of activity of which we should be aware. Some things may make us feel driven; others may bring us joy or pleasure or perhaps a mix of both.

It is the same with things for children. Karen can remember tracing joined-up writing in a book of endless joined-up letters with no meaning. It was so boring, and she hated it. Why did she have to do it when she could write already, even if without being joined up? Things that children possess and bring to school can illuminate poverty or wealth of the child and lead to envy, sadness, disappointment or glee, none of which is desirable. In Karen's kindergarten there was a beautiful grey rocking horse called Misty, with long hair for its mane and a long tail. It was very inviting, but it soon became the object of hard-fought battles about whose turn it was to ride it, so it became anathema to Karen, who chose to stay away from Misty, just watching the others.

Place

Cresswell (2015) describes how place is more than geography:

> But place is also a way of seeing, knowing, and understanding the world. When we look at the world of places, we see different things. We see attachments and connections between people and place. We see worlds of meaning and experience.
>
> (Cresswell, 2015, p. 18)

Place is linked to our sense of identity. Home is described by Cresswell as an exemplary kind of space, where people feel, we hope, a sense of attachment and rootedness. Home is a centre of meaning and a place of care. It is also a place where one can withdraw and have respite from the world outside. We suggest that these dimensions of home need to apply to school as well, especially if home for the child does not live up to these standards. Home, and we argue school, is a gathering of things, memories, stories, and practices. It is full of things and is a unique assemblage that is different every day. Belonging is another key concept underpinning place. Skillman (2020) suggests that many have argued that a sense of belonging is at the core of self-esteem. In 'Belonging: A Culture of Place,' bell hooks interprets belonging as a place where the soul can rest (hooks, 2009, in Cooper, 2020).

Places are socially constructed; buildings and playgrounds take a particular form. Schools are traditionally fenced off from the rest of the community. The school has been built with a notion of how it should look and be experienced. The classroom as a place isn't just the walls and furniture but rather the whole experience that results from the way people inhabit it, and how they inhabit it is influenced by identities they have already created in other places (Ellis, 2005).

The identity of a place itself also contributes to its meaning for those inside it. In part, a place develops its significance or identity through stories about what has happened there (Ellis, 2005). For example, if a school has a strong reputation for certain kinds of accomplishments, such as sports or music, it already has an identity.

Place embraces, we hope, both security and freedom. If classrooms are to be good places, we suggest they should provide, building on Ellis's (2005) ideas, safety, nurturance, positive relationships with peers and adults and opportunities for positive identities, while including space for children's creative self-development.

Over time children may develop a greater sense of place in a classroom or school. If their experiences in these places are filled with familiar routines that build their confidence – if they know and become known by others, acquire intimate local knowledge and learn the norms of the culture – then sense of place may be well established. However, be it positive or negative in nature, the classroom and school will acquire an emotional significance for them. As teachers who want, we suggest, children's classroom experiences to be positive, we must consider whether the classroom affords social comfort and belonging, creative self-development, and positive identities (Ellis, 2005).

You have probably heard of attachment theory in an emotional child development context, but Langhout (2004), in a review of children and place research, reported that autonomy, social support and positive feelings are associated with children's place attachment or sense of place. An example of autonomy is choosing a book from a selection. Social support may be a trusted person managing the break time. Positive feelings may result from the teacher praising good work in the classroom.

As a teacher, you have responsibility for most of the things, rules, routines and activities that will shape the everyday lives of children in your class. The relationships students develop will both result from, and contribute to, everyday life. The relationships are important, as these will support or fail to support community and positive identities for students. If students become confident with familiar routines, come to know and be known by their peers and have intimate knowledge about the course experience, then they may well establish a sense of belonging in the classroom.

Theatres of learning

Sara Johnston described to Karen how a team in her school developed 'theatres of learning.' Before the first day of school, schoolteachers explored charity shops, lofts and DIY shops to create a theatre of learning. One such place was a pirates' galleon for the children to inhabit on their first day at school. The reaction of the children was one of awe and wonder. Project learning was linked to the new environment and also linked into parents and the wider community, to enter into the spirit of the new theatre for learning.

Time

In their research into thinking time, Moxnes and Aslanian (2022) discuss the tyranny of time, which can govern learning, relationships and curriculum planning rather than fostering a curiosity about what teachers and children can do together. But, we ask, how can teachers think about children's time to think and to learn if outside pressures makes it difficult for them to think themselves? With the current emphasis laid on coverage of curriculum content, there is a perceived rush to be 'on time.' The more external aims teachers work to meet, the less time is devoted to listening to and observing children, and this withdrawn time also reduces children's and teachers' possibilities for thinking and for thoughtfulness.

Rowe's (1974) research highlighted the fact that many teachers leave less than one second after asking a question, if no answer is forthcoming, before asking another question or answering their own question. The key to changing such a situation is to allow a longer 'wait time.' However, even with short wait times, the only questions that work are those that can be answered quickly, without thought – that is, questions that call for memorized facts.

Black and Wiliam (2004), in their work on putting assessment into practice, noticed that some teachers expected all their pupils to be able to answer a question at any time, even if that answer were 'I don't know.' The teachers had to establish an atmosphere where children were comfortable giving a wrong answer so that they and their classmates could explore the 'wrong' answer. 'Put simply, the only point of asking questions is to raise issues about which the teacher needs information or about which the pupils need to think' (Black & Wiliam, 2004, p. 27). Many teachers found silences stressful but learned, over time, to reflect more on the type of questions they asked – questions that would promote deeper thinking in the children.

Odegard (2021, p. 74) emphasizes the importance of slowing down 'to give time for entanglements and deepening of thoughts, ideas, phenomena, time for formulating, time for listening and time for becoming.' Dewey (1933, p. 3) believed that 'thinking … consists in turning a subject over in the mind and giving it serious and consecutive consideration.' And this applies to both adult and child.

But teachers also need time for reflection.

Time: Time to make sense of things

Alison had a conversation with former colleagues Lynne and Morag.

Alison: How important is time for the child?

Lynne: So, are we talking about time in terms of learning … learning about the world? Well … time to settle and time to think, certainly … time to revisit and repeat.

Morag: I think if I were to organise my learning environment again, I'd be much more aware of the child who perhaps thinks, I haven't learnt this today, and I'm never going to learn it … I think I would be very keen to explore the child's thinking … so, OK … it's not going to happen today, it might not happen next week, but one of those days, it's going to make sense … other things will happen to make it make sense for you … and I would put parameters both in time and space. … We all do our best to ensure our children's learning, but I didn't share with them this understanding that it's not always going to be like this. (Clicks her fingers). It's (learning) a process.

Lynne: I can think of one thing that kind of illustrates that. … Woodside Primary, P2 … in May, when they did the assessment of their reading ability (it was a screening thing that went on every year; it would identify children who needed additional support), and I remember Rose going into the class and explaining to the children that she was going to listen to their reading and this little thing they were going to do together. They went, '"Oh, Sandy's the reader!' because there was one child in the class who was good at reading, came from the same kind of background, but he was a reader...read beautifully...and they had identified that. She gave them all the test and screened them all ... now that was P2 ... two years later, one of those children, the one who pointed Sandy out as 'the reader', not identifying himself as a reader, was walking along the corridor and suddenly realised that the word that was up on the wall heading to the TV room and said, 'Miss, miss, that says ...' and all of a sudden realised that he could recognise the words. That took two years for him, despite the fact that there would have been reading going on in that class daily.

Morag: And the space to make mistakes ... try things out ... try again. I'm thinking of my own experiences as a young learner, and really the whole thing was circumscribed. You sat in your seat and you learned. But, just occasionally, the headteacher, who was of the old school and had all sorts of difficulties, PTSD (posttraumatic stress disorder), I suspect ... he would take us out and he would say, if we were learning about triangles, 'Now, you've come down from the glebe today and you came across the fields, you took a short-cut. Think of the triangle that goes up to the corner. ... He walked out the triangle with and for us. And, occasionally, did something like that which made sense and made these links with the real world of our learning, away from that seat where you were sitting, with someone looking over your shoulder to see that you're doing it correctly ... and you don't have that space to make mistakes, or to think, or to consolidate.

In essence, both Lynne and Morag were advocating a focus on the creation of opportunities for the children 'to roam the known,' to relate their new learning to life outside the classroom and to make sense of what it is they have learned. Learning is a process that is piecemeal, gradual and needs to be revisited again and again until the learning is secure.

Learning Points

1. Learning is an iterative process.
2. The physical and emotional place of the classroom matters to children.
3. Fostering a sense of belonging is crucial for both the children and the teacher.
4. Time needs to be devoted to listening to and observing children so that we know where they are in the learning space.
5. Children need space and time to make mistakes and to try things out repeatedly.

Challenge Questions

1. As a teacher, how can you make the place and space comfortable for the children?
2. What are the differences for a child between home and school? Much time in a child's life is spent in both places.

3. How can home and school coordinate or communicate to enhance a child's life experience?
4. How can safety, security and freedom be made present for the children in your classroom?

References

Black, P., & Wiliam, D. (2004). The formative purpose: Assessment must first promote learning. *Yearbook of the National Society for the Study of Education* 103(2), 20-50.

Cooper, J.A. (2020). Belonging: A culture of place by bell hooks. *Southeastern Geographer* 60(4), 360-362.

Cresswell, T. (2015). *Place: An introduction*, 2nd ed. Wiley Blackwell, Chichester, West Sussex, UK.

Dewey, J. (1933). *How we think*. Dover Publications, Boston, MA.

Ellis, J. (2005). Place and identity for children in classrooms and schools. *Journal of the Canadian Association for Curriculum Studies* 3(2).

Fenwick, T., & Edwards, R. (2010). *Actor-network theory in education*. Routledge, London.

Langhout, R.D. (2004). Facilitators and inhibitors of positive school feelings: An exploratory study. *American Journal of Community Psychology* 34(1-2), 111-127.

Moxnes, A.R., & Aslanian, T.K. (2022). Thinking time: Producing time and toddler's time to think. In ECEC *Global Studies of Childhood 2022* 12(3), 277-328.

Odegard, N. (2021). Aesthetic explorations with recycled materials: Concepts, ideas and phenomena that matter. *Skriftserien (2021)*. oslomet.no

Rowe, M.B. (1974). Wait time and rewards as instructional variables, their influence on language, logic and fate control. *Journal of Research in Science Teaching*, 11, 81-94.

Skillman, A.E. (2020). Building community self-esteem: Advocating for culture. *Folklore*, 131(3), 229-243. https://doi.org/10.1080/0015587X.2020.1772577

10 Wellbeing

Introduction

Wellbeing is a widely used term that is rarely defined. The Organisation for Economic Co-operation and Development (OECD/Carnegie, 2016) describe different dimensions of wellbeing with adults in mind. They cite:

- Health;
- Safety;
- Housing;
- Access to services;
- Education;
- Jobs;
- Environment;
- Income.

We suggest the spiritual dimension is missing. All of these, or lack of these for adults, would affect children too. For children we would add the need for play, joy, creativity, wonder, possibility and imagination. Karen's definition in her research on wellbeing and our definition for this chapter is:

> Living a life of value for self and others.

This definition recognises that wellbeing is different for everyone, and it also has an impact on others, so it cannot be entirely hedonistic. Health is important to wellbeing, but 90% of health determinants are not health-system related but are social and economic (Kilpatrick, 2009). Studies suggest that the majority of 'engaged' individuals perceive that there are benefits for their physical health, psychological health, self-confidence, self-esteem, sense of personal empowerment and social relationships (Milton et al., 2011). Engagement or getting involved is clearly important to the wellbeing of adults, and we propose for children too.

The purposes of education

Spratt (2018) discusses the purposes of education and whether this is linked to wellbeing. She asks the question, does education serve economic purposes or does it serve to enhance personal freedom? Whereas the more complex and interesting question she suggests is, how do these facets of education interact? It is clear that tensions exist between the purposes, and that problems emerge when the economic targets of education are allowed to overshadow other aims. Rather than seeing the different purposes of education as contradictory, Biesta (2009) argues that education has composite purposes. He suggested three different, related functions of education: qualification (skills, knowledge and dispositions that allow a person to do something), socialisation (teaching individuals how to adopt existing norms, values and ways of doing things), and subjectification (providing opportunities for unique qualities of individuals to come 'into presence,' p. 80).

Socialisation and subjectification are seen to be the opposite of each other, as socialisation is guiding children towards similar traits, so they can 'fit in' to contemporary society, whereas subjectification values and fosters the individuality of children (Spratt, 2018). Wellbeing is often portrayed as an alternative to an attainment-driven curriculum, removing the focus from learning outcomes to the holistic development of the 'whole child' (Spratt, 2018).

The policy identifies eight 'indicators of wellbeing,' which are described as 'the basic requirements for all children and young people to grow and develop and reach their full potential'. (Scottish Government, 2012, p. 10). The indicators are safe, healthy, achieving, nurtured, active, respected, responsible and included, often referred to collectively with the acronym SHANARRI in Scotland and are represented in Figure 10.1. The wording on each sector of the model is phrased in terms of the adult responsibility in conferring the rights; for example 'having help to overcome' difficulties, being 'protected from abuse,' being 'guided and supported in learning' or 'having opportunities to take part in activities such as play.' This model locates deficits in the environment rather than the child and represents the role of professionals in working together to ensure that a nurturing environment is in place (Spratt, 2018).

Thinking and reflecting about wellbeing

Löhre et al. (2010) describe research that shows that wellbeing is related to children's experiences with teachers. Their research suggested, in contrast to other studies, peer experiences such as being bullied or being lonely were less significant. In addition, children's reports of teacher likeability (how nice they think their teachers are) seem to be important for their school satisfaction. There were also gender differences, with girls having a better relationship with teachers and a poorer, less positive attitude towards school. You might like to think whether and why this should be the case. For instance, are schools designed in ways which suit boys' wellbeing more than the wellbeing of girls?

Clarke and Platt (2023) distinguish in their research between wellbeing feelings (hedonia) and wellbeing functioning (eudaimonia), concluding that both are important. In contrast to the study by Löhre, Clarke and Platt (2023) conclude that children's experiences of 'feeling good' at school were characterised by an interdependence on peers' emotional states (described as 'a domino effect'), a need to feel cared for by, and trust towards, adults and a desire for autonomy over their time. Children attributed mistrust in adults when adults disregarded seemingly incidental events that felt significant to the children. Children experienced 'doing well' as equating to academic attainment, conveying a fixation with test scores and

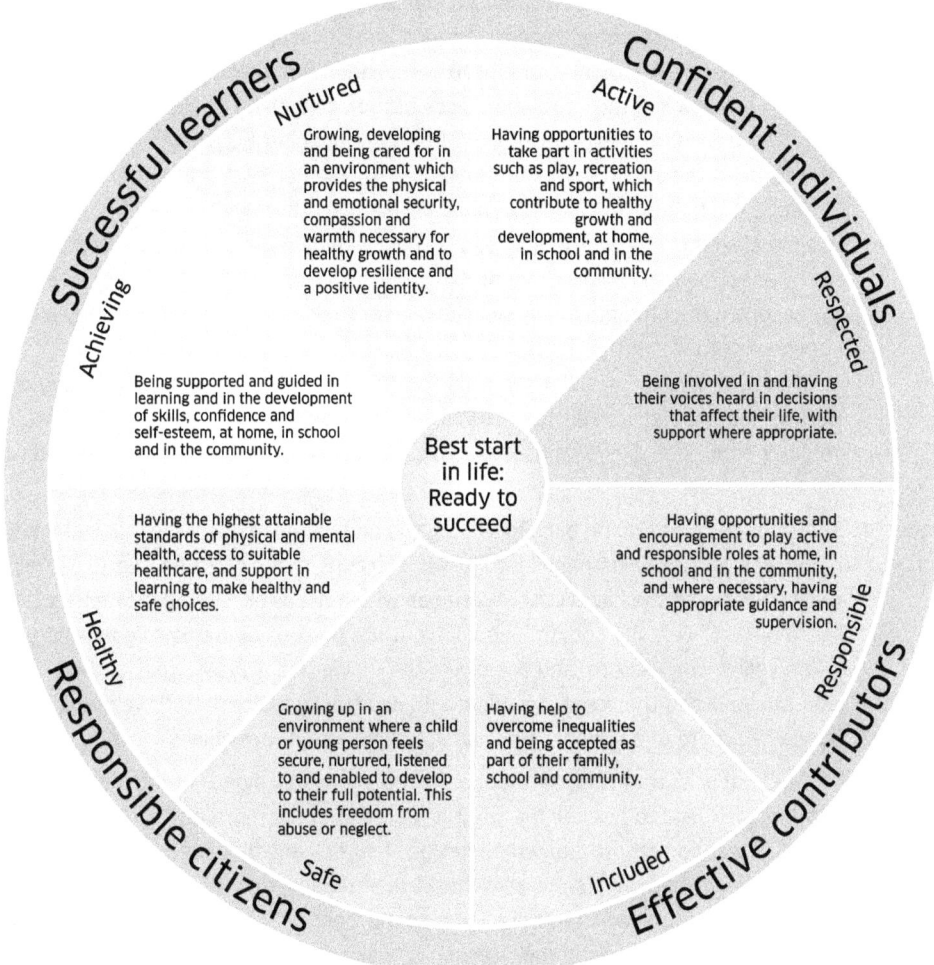

Figure 10.1 GIRFEC's wellbeing wheel (Scottish Government, 2012, p. 10)

using language of 'correctness' and efficiency. Shame pervaded when 'correctness' was not achieved, with children describing being ridiculed for poor test results.

And so we meet Lily, in primary 4 (age 8-9). Ellie and Paul, her parents, describe their concerns for her with Alison:

Ellie: As she grew, obviously the demands of school changed. We kind of thought, well, she's conforming, she's doing as she's told and things are changing. Academically she was fine, no problems. She does what she's told. So, when did it happen? Post Covid? 2020? This was another point in Lily's timeline. The teacher had put a movie on.... the premise of the movie was that the parents were taken away from the child and they lived in this alternative dimension..... almost like Covid in a movie, wasn't it? They lived in their house and there was a secret door in their house that took them through to this different world. It was an animated movie and I think perhaps now that with all the heightened emotions and uncertainty, she just did not cope with it well and the movie traumatised her..... and then just changed the course of the next few years. It took away her sense of the world being a safe place. The alternative world where the parents were fun and engaging but they had like button eyes...... so in the end, this fun family wanted to take her away from her real family.

And it wasn't just Lily, was it? There were a few other kids as well that also had trouble sleeping afterwards and had to check their mum and dad's eyes before they went to bed and all that sort of thing. She was eight. They were going to watch the second half of the movie the next day. And she did say, we watched a movie and I don't want to watch the rest.

That summer her behaviour was just erratic. We had no idea what was going on. Because she still struggled to verbalise things from the experience back in P1. It couldn't come out. She was having panic attacks which seemed like they'd come out of nowhere.

Paul: Then when she was going back to school, she had her head down the toilet, she was being sick and she was panicking. It was extreme, really extreme. We eventually realised because she had a school cardigan with buttons on - in the movie they had these button eyes, she couldn't even look at the buttons on her cardigan. And you had a yellow coat, Alison, and the girl in the movie had a yellow coat and she was like ... I can't see that coat. So eventually we tracked it back and we're like, this movie had more of an impact than we actually thought possible.

Ellie: In the October of that year, we met the headteacher. Lily didn't want to come to the meeting, so I said to her, tell me what it feels like in the morning before you go to school. It was something along the lines of, I feel sick and dizzy and wobbly. My legs don't work. My body hurts. We said this at the meeting, and the teacher said, 'well, that's that then ... we'll temporarily suspend her. We'll have to get social work involved.' We didn't understand. They said, 'well she's fine at school.'

Paul: Well, of course she's fine at school because she behaves. She wants to fit in. We didn't know at the time, but she was masking wonderfully well, as children do at times. But then when she came home, it was a safe place. It's where she could relax and you know, cry to Kate or shout at us. She became all sorts, didn't we? Violent and aggressive, almost like an alter ego of the child we had known. All the time the school was saying, 'you have to bring her in, you have to bring her to school. You've got to keep her coming in.' It was like this doesn't seem humane to do this to someone. ...

Ellie: Resilience was a word that was brought up, and if you don't bring her to school, she won't have any resilience because she won't have pushed through, she won't have had these experiences.

Paul: We don't believe that you need to break through something to make someone more resilient. We think resilience is something you learn over time by understanding yourself and understanding your own levels and limits, that sort of thing. We had lots of meetings, didn't' we? And after the meetings, we'd come out and say, brilliant, great, we understand where they are and they understand where we are,

	they're going to put this in place, we're going to do this, we're going to do that … and then, nothing was done. Nothing changed.
Ellie:	They commented on my anxiety about Lily and said I needed to control my anxiety and the most important thing was to bring her in regardless of how she was behaving, as they put it. And so, at the end of the meeting, I was like, thank you, this all sounds really great. And then I got home and I broke down. I just felt awful because it was like they ended up pushing it back on me, saying, 'Well, if you just manage your anxiety a bit better, then perhaps we could get her back into school. And once she's here, she's fine. We're not going to change anything to suit her; she'll be fine when she's here.' The whole thing was dressed up as being in Lily's best interest. But it wasn't.
Paul:	That just didn't connect with us at all.
Ellie:	There were times when we said to each other, how can we put our child in an environment where they're supposed to be in loco parentis – where they're supposed to be in charge of our human being and meeting her needs, keeping her safe, when we don't trust that's what they're doing at all?
Alison:	Surely those teachers couldn't have been me or any of the teachers I've worked with over many years. Surely not?

Clarke and Platt (2023) describe factors that have an impact on children's wellbeing.

Together-apart

Children described experiences of being together and apart as making them 'feel good' or 'less good,' including their happiness being dependent on friends' happiness, 'connecting'/ playing with friends, inclusion/exclusion, making 'new' friends and school being their central source of friendship.

A pen can be stronger than a sword

Children shared a range of experiences of being victims of cruelty from 'being bullied' to peers talking 'about you behind your back,' 'passing notes,' saying 'mean things' or feeling humiliated when they get a 'question wrong' and 'the whole school knows.'

It feels like they don't care

Some children expressed feeling that adults at school did not care about them, describing different experiences that had led them to believe this, in contrast to the kindness of friends who showed they cared through words of appreciation.

They could maybe help a little bit more

Feeling helpless or frustrated characterised many children's experiences of school, with many longing for individual support and feedback on their schoolwork from teachers:

People around you got it all right

Children described feelings of shame when their answers were incorrect, frequently comparing their 'correctness' to others' expectations and expressing a desire for social validation.

A UK Government-commissioned review of 397 UK-specific studies exploring children's experiences of wellbeing (Dex & Hollingworth, 2012) identified three central themes: relationships (feeling loved and cared for); self and freedoms (freedom from bullying and school-related stress and need for autonomy); and environment (access to services and resources).

Critiques of wellbeing

Some commentators on wellbeing in education believe the introduction of wellbeing into school policy has been dominated by a conception of an individualised set of physical, social and emotional skills and responsibilities that children are expected to enact or internalise. As Spratt (2018) describes, this approach carries assumptions of 'one size fits all,' as it portrays one correct way of feeling and being, ignoring the individual, cultural and experiential differences between children and taking no account of how children themselves might understand their wellbeing. It may be seen, as Spratt suggests, that schools are invited to work with children in order to 'remedy' feelings that may be seen as negative.

Nussbaum (2006) argues that education must focus on freedom of the mind. Rejecting forms of learning that focus solely on predetermined outcomes or are over-reliant on memory, she argues that, 'education must begin with the mind of the child and it must have a goal for increasing that mind's freedom in its social environment rather than killing it off' (p. 393). She encourages pedagogical approaches that encourage critical thinking (See Chapter 16: Moving forward) that promote democracy through an awareness of 'world citizenship' and narrative imagination, cultured through artistic and expressive education. In order to support children and young people to be able to make well-informed and rational choices about those things that are of value in life, they need to be provided with opportunities to develop their critical powers of analysis and to understand the implications of their choices for others.

Simmons (2015) conducted research asking students and teachers to imagine and describe an ideal school for wellbeing; this was understandably grounded in their current experience of school. A 'wellbeing school' began to emerge, she states, sometimes with rather utopian features. These imaginary schools had a strong grounding in communal values, such as sharing, respect, cooperation, participation and equality, as well as identifying resources to support the students' wellbeing needs. Such values were reflected within and across the four major themes that emerged in the data from both primary and secondary students, specifically concerning improvements to (1) pedagogy, (2) school environment, (3) relationships, and (4) opportunities to have a say.

1. The students discussed wanting practical ways to learn, such as learning about safety through caring for dangerous animals and learning from doing and watching. As one student stated, 'make movies at our school for watching things to help you learn'. The students in years 5-6 (10-12 years old) discussed similar ideas but emphasised features such as 'outside learning,' 'individual help on certain subjects,' 'different ways to do a

subject,' 'hands-on work,' 'fun learning activities,' 'different activities to find out what learner you are' and 'students should write down what they want to learn about and why.' These students also put a strong emphasis on the role of their teacher in facilitating their learning.
2. The desire for natural space was also evident across all participants, and especially for the year 1-2 cohort (5-6 years), who viewed nature as integral to 'having fun' in their wellbeing school. Their drawings incorporated shady trees, sunshine, flowers, beaches and animals. The students also conveyed the desire for further facilities to be added to the natural environment, such as 'play swings,' 'a jumping castle,' and outdoor swimming pools and water slides. These were used to further convey the importance students placed on having fun and being happy at school.
3. Relationships featured strongly across all cohorts. The year 1-2 students imagined improved, caring, dispute-free relationships with teachers, the principal, and friends, as well as competent teachers who could mediate conflict. In addition, there was a strong focus on the emotional support provided through relationships at school, such as feeling loved, safe, happy and cared for.
4. Given the research was designed to provide students (and teachers) with the opportunity to express their views, it is not altogether surprising to find a strong theme for student wellbeing in the data around the importance of having opportunities to have a say. While this theme was not as evident in data from the year 1-2 students, the year 5-6 (ages 10-11) students emphasised the importance of 'voice' in having a say regarding school procedures, such as 'being allowed to sit with friends,' 'you're allowed to be in the same class as your friend,' 'allowed to choose your teacher,' and 'students get asked on how the school should be run.'

Creativity and the arts

The World Health Organisation (WHO) produced a report on evidence of the arts in improving health and wellbeing. Research studies were included on theories from psychology, psychiatry, epidemiology, philosophy, ecology, history, health economics, neuroscience, medicine, health geography, public health, anthropology and sociology among others, which shows the complexity and reach of the arts in our lives.

Additionally, this review identified how the arts can provide a holistic lens to view conditions that are often treated primarily as physical; this approach fits with current trends in health towards giving parity of esteem to mental health and also towards situating health problems within their social and community context.

> Health is a state of complete physical, mental and social wellbeing and not merely an absence of disease or infirmity.
>
> (World Health Organisation, 1946)

This is a rather static but helpful definition, and a more dynamic one is based on the resilience or capacity to cope and maintain and restore one's integrity, equilibrium and sense of wellbeing (Huber et al., 2011; Clift & Camic, 2016).

The arts may be defined in many ways, but we like the description by Clift and Camic (2016): 'the arts are heart, are about creativity and problem-solving, and above all about helping to create both meaning and a sense of beauty in all our lives' (p. 9). Clift and Camic further cite Gardner and Gardner (2011): What is true, what is good and what is beautiful are central to the educational enterprise and should be the heart of any balanced curriculum.

It is impossible here to do justice to this topic of the link between arts and wellbeing; the topic is both interesting and important. One example must suffice. Theorell and Ullén (2016) describe how musical experiences and early musical training stimulate general cognitive development. They cite research that shows links have been made to speech perception, verbal, auditory and visual memory, vocabulary, reading ability, visuo-spatial abilities and general IQ.

Karen's Aunt Barbara, who is currently in her 90s, remembers a time when artistic skills were required of teachers to enter primary school teacher training. She played piano, and this was consistently used throughout her career. Everyone can manage artistic creativity at some level, and this is crucial to rounded wellbeing in education.

Learning points

1. Wellbeing is different for everyone.
2. Some approaches portray wellbeing as one correct way of feeling and being, ignoring the individual, cultural and experiential differences between children.
3. We need to consider how children themselves might understand their wellbeing.
4. Children's experiences of 'feeling good' include a need to feel cared for by, and trust towards, adults and a desire for a say in their school routine.
5. Economic targets for education can overshadow other aims.
6. The importance of the arts and creativity for wellbeing should not be ignored.

Challenge questions

1. What is your reaction to parents Ellie and Paul's opinions about Lily's education?
2. How can and do you educate the whole child?
3. What arts skills do you have or use in your teaching practice?

References

Biesta, G. (2009). Good education in an age of measurement: On the need to reconnect with the question of purpose in education. *Educational Assessment, Evaluation and Accountability*, 21(1), 33-46.

Clarke, T., & Platt, R. (2023). Children's lived experiences of wellbeing at school in England: A phenomenological inquiry. *Child Indicators Research*, 16, 963-996.

Clift, S., & Camic, P.M. (2016). Introduction to the field of creative arts, wellbeing, and health: Achievements and current challenges. In *Oxford textbook of creative arts, health and Wellbeing: International perspectives on practice, policy, and research*, pp. 3-10. Oxford University Press, Oxford.

Dex, S. and Hollingworth, K., (2012). *Children's and young people's voices on their wellbeing*. Childhood Wellbeing Research Centre, London.

Gardner, H. and Gardner, G., (2011). *Truth, beauty, and goodness reframed: Educating for the virtues in the twenty-first century*. Basic Books, New York.

Huber, M., Knotterus, J., & van der Horst, H. (2011). How should we define health? *British Medical Journal*, 343, 1-3.

Kilpatrick, S. (2009). Multi-level rural community engagement in health. *Australian Journal of Rural Health*, 17, 39-44.

Löhre, A., Lydersen, S., & Vatten, L. (2010). School wellbeing among children in grades 1-10. *BMC Public Health*, 10, 526. http://www.biomedcentral.com/1471-2458/10/526

Milton, B., Attree, P., French, B., Povall, S., Whitehead, M., & Popay, J. (2011, June 23). The impact of community engagement on health and social outcomes: A systematic review. *Community Development Journal Advance Access*.

Nussbaum, M.C. (2006). Education and democratic citizenship: Capabilities and quality education. *Journal of Human Development*, 7(3), 385-395. https://doi.org/10.1080/14649880600815974

OECD/Carnegie UK. (2016). *Sharpening our focus: Guidance on wellbeing frameworks for cities and regions*. Carnegie Trust, Dunfermline, Scotland.

Scottish Government. (2012). *GIRFEC's wellbeing wheel*. Scottish Government, Edinburgh.

Simmons, C., Graham, A., & Thomas, N. (2015). Imagining an ideal school for wellbeing: Locating student voice. *Journal of Educational Change*, 16, 129-144.

Spratt, J. (2018). Health and wellbeing. In T.G.K. Bryce, W.M. Humes, D. Gillies, & A. Kennedy (Eds.), *Scottish Education*. Edinburgh University Press, 2018, pp. 527-532. https://doi.org/10.1515/9781474437851-062

Theorell, T., & Ullén, F. (2016). Epidemiological studies of the relationship between cultural experiences and public health. In S. Clift & P. Camic (Eds.), *Oxford textbook of creative arts, health and wellbeing: International perspectives on practice, policy and research*. Oxford University Press, Oxford, UK.

World Health Organisation. (1946). *Preamble to the Constitution of the WHO, as adopted by the International Health Conference, New York, 19-22 June, 1946*. Official Record of the WHO, No. 2 (p. 100).

World Health Organisation. (undated). What is the evidence on the role of the arts in improving health and well-being? A scoping review. *Health Evidence Network Synthesis Report 67*. Copenhagen, Denmark.

11 Nurturing

> To take care of, feed, and protect someone or something, especially young children or plants, and help him, her, or it to develop.
>
> (Cambridge Dictionary Online, accessed 4 November, 2024)

Metaphors for teaching often feature the nurturing of plants, perhaps through rich soil or regular watering. This can be criticised, as the agency is in the teacher doing the watering, when it is the child who is doing the growing and developing. It is, however, a positive metaphor in that it relates to the natural way of the world and has ecological connotations.

Nurturing or caring?

Noddings, in her book *Caring* (1984), described a relational and reciprocal view of caring. The cared-for child recognises the caring and responds in some detectable manner. For example, an infant smiles and wriggles in response to its mother's caregiving. Similarly, a child may acknowledge the teacher's caring directly by saying 'thank you' or by simply pursuing their own work more confidently. The receptive teacher can see that their caring has been received by monitoring their children's responses. Of foremost importance is placing the child as a priority and nurturing the child-teacher relationship in 'receptivity, relatedness, and responsiveness' (1984,p. 2).

Hayes and Filipović (2018) suggest the term 'caring' is not sufficient:

> the word nurture provides a more engaging and active image than the word care; it conveys a more engaged level of interaction and requires the adult to actively nourish, rear, foster, train and educate the child through his/her practice.
>
> (Hayes & Filipović, 2018, p. 222)

It is our belief that nurture is the right of all children, of all ages and in all classes. And it is the responding, encouraging, smiling, reflecting and so forth by the teacher that helps the child to engage and be engaged in their learning. (See Chapter 14 on Rights). Exploring nurturing in education on the internet, we found:

> Some examples of nurturing behaviour are: being fully present in your interactions with children (verbally and non-verbally), validating their feelings, providing physical affection and comfort when sought, laughing and playing games, providing safe mental, physical and social challenges that promote healthy growth …

DOI: 10.4324/9781032678283-14

A nurturing approach to education focuses on the emotional and social needs of children and young people, in addition to their academic learning. It's based on the idea that positive relationships are central to learning and wellbeing, and that early experiences have a significant impact on development.
(Google search for 'education, nurturing'. Accessed 04 November, 2024)

Nurturing is often associated with very young children, but we believe it is relevant to the education of all ages, including adults. Following is a story of school transitions from Penny, clearly for older children.

During Covid times, post lockdown, our school returned to full time face-to-face teaching. Because it had been difficult for many children and families, we thought it was really important to develop ways of nurturing the children on a daily basis. We used daily notebooks, for the children to record their thoughts, wishes, and feelings, as their early morning activity.

They would have a daily question based on the day of the week. For example, Wonderful Wednesday – what is wonderful about you? Thoughtful Thursday – who do you know is thoughtful and why?

Nurturing and transition to high school

An important part of the transition to high school, another area, or a different country for all children is to ensure their feelings of wellbeing are maintained. A crucial part of a child's development is to develop through nurture a more stable mental state, which helps them to live stable lives as adults.

Two different examples of transition to high school: Successful and unsuccessful

Martin was in the process of being diagnosed with ADHD in his final year at primary school. He was intelligent, fun, sporty, yet often disruptive in class. Although attempts were made to set up more transition sessions to his new high school, this never came to fruition. His class teacher had one short phone call with a staff member who wanted to know Martin's grades. Unfortunately, Martin was given three detentions in his first week, and his behaviour continued to spiral downward leading to his suspension in his first term. He arrived at the primary school gate during his first term asking to help with football practice because he wanted to come back.

Laura was in foster care, where her carers were actively involved in all aspects of her welfare. She too was in the process of being diagnosed with ADHD. The process of transition to high school started 6 months before she left primary school. In contrast to Martin's transition, Laura was able to familiarise herself with the staff, buildings and workings of her new school on separate, individual visits. She had a successful first term, where she was accepted and nurtured really well by staff with whom she came into contact. Although her behaviour in class was similar to Martin's in primary school, her needs had been fully addressed at her new high school. She received awards and certificates and was given added responsibilities to help develop her self-esteem.

Nurture groups: The six guiding principles

As far back as 1970, nurture groups were established in the UK to provide a nurturing approach for children and young people to engage with missing early nurturing experiences, giving them the social and emotional skills to do well at school and with peers, and to develop their resilience and self-confidence. This approach encouraged pupils to take pride in achieving by addressing the social and emotional needs that can hamper learning, through the introduction of short-term interventions for children with emotional, social, behavioural and learning needs. Nurture groups are a short-term, focused intervention strategy to support young people (primary school years 1-3; ages 5-8) who have attachment-related social, behavioural, emotional and wellbeing needs that could otherwise become long-term barriers to learning and attainment. Nurture groups are small classes of between 8 and 12 children based in mainstream schools, that provide a short-term intervention for children with social, emotional and learning needs (Boxall, 2002).

McNicol and Reilly (2015) describe the six guiding principles of nurture.

1. Learning is understood developmentally.
2. The classroom offers a safe base.
3. Nurture is important for the development of self-esteem (wellbeing).
4. Language is understood as a vital means of communication.
5. All behaviour is communication.
6. Transitions are significant in the lives of children.

Key nurture group researchers were influenced by attachment theory. For example, Bennathan and Boxall (2000) claimed that a child's early social and cognitive development stems from early nurturing care that centres on attachment and involves the close identification of parent and child. This constitutes the first stage of development through which children begin to learn and interact with others. Children's difficulties may be understood in terms of impoverished experiences of nurture in early life (Morris, 2018). They may lack the early learning experiences that usually occur through a 'trusting relationship with an attentive and responsive parent' (Boxall, 2002, p. 1). As children who attend nurture groups may not have had access to responsive adults at home, it is particularly important that they build secure attachments with nurture staff (Boxall, 2002).

Morris describes how children learn from nurture groups. Children learn about friendship as they play together. They make friends as they develop shared interests and joy in play activities. As they play, children become more aware of others, more sensitive towards others and develop a greater understanding of the feelings of others. This also has wider implications as it has been argued that learning about friendships through play helps children to form representations of social relationships in the wider social world (Morris, 2018).

Nurture staff offer what is termed by Morris (2018) as 'compensatory mothering,' with reference to examples of them taking action to meet the physical and emotional needs of the children. We, the authors, feel uncomfortable using the term 'mothering,' as the teacher is *not* the mother and does not go home with the children after school. It also excludes the notion of 'fathering.' Morris, however, focuses on the ways in which the domestic environment supports the notion of mothering. I have referred to the ways in which groups have been set up to contain features of home as well as school, in line with recommended nurture group practice (Boxall, 2002). Examples of the ways in which the staff provide activities that would usually take place at home include baking and sharing breakfast, and examples of the ways in which the staff focus on teaching skills that would usually be taught in the home include learning good manners and self-help skills (Morris, 2018).

There is a link between the notion of mothering and attachment theory, according to Morris (Morris, 2018). It has commonly been claimed that the staff in nurture groups become attachment figures for the children. We suggest this is probably the case in any classroom, to some degree, where the teacher is welcoming and nurturing. However, Morris has explored the notion of mothering as part of a social process. Morris's findings have added to the research relating to a link between mothering and teaching. Whilst some have reported that teaching has been seen as an extension of mothering, her research supports a view of mothering as pedagogy. Morris also found in her research that the nurture staff provided emotional scaffolding during interactions involving high levels of attention and praise.

Whilst Morris (2018) argued for a balance between child-led models of play and more structured, teacher-led models, she also identified missed opportunities in terms of adults becoming involved in play in which the children have set the agenda. Joining in with children's play could help to strengthen relationships between the children and nurture staff, as well as providing opportunities for the co-construction of meaning.

Play in nurture groups

Whilst play in nurture groups has often been viewed developmentally, Morris's research has explored the social processes involved in play. She describes how children enjoy having adults as play partners. They seek attention as they try to involve adults in their play and form relationships through play-based interactions. However, a key finding was that the extent to which the nurture staff engage in play depended on the play context. Whilst they always prioritised play, Morris found that they sometimes appeared to be uncertain about the nature of the play opportunities that should be offered and their roles in relation to play. After a discussion of the theory around child-initiated play and adult-led play, Morris concluded that both types of play are beneficial to children in nurture groups.

Morris also describes how children create social worlds as they play with their peers and that children form friendships and construct representations of wider social relationships as they play together. She also claims that children make sense of their home lives and family relationships as they engage in domestic play with their peers. This has corroborated the view that children actively construct meaning in relation to their world through play.

We, the authors, have a concern about stigma and nurture groups and questions about who decides which children are to be in a nurture group. Following, Alison describes a child she knew called Kris who went to nurture group.

Kris is 8 years old and is in primary 4 in a small rural primary school. He is a happy wee boy at home with a vast range of interests: reading, drawing, swimming and talking to any adult who will listen to him. But his interests are solitary. He finds difficulty in socialising with his peers at school and difficulty in maintaining his concentration, and he is 'fidgety'.

He is currently in the process of being checked for a diagnosis of attention deficit hyperactivity disorder (ADHD).

There is a nurturing group in his school, which he has been attending in the morning, but his parents are anxious about the apparent stigma of being excluded from his composite class, whose curricular work he enjoys. The school has been equally willing to ensure that his particular needs are being met and that his parents' wishes are also being met. In the first instance, Kris was offered the choice of whether he wanted to go to the nurture group or to remain in class.

Things changed when a new teacher was appointed to the school and to his class. Her area of expertise and particular interest was working with children with additional support needs. She believes in the right of all children to be involved in decision-making about their learning environment – that they should all feel safe and happy.

In the first week of the new term, the children arrived to an empty classroom: No posters on the walls, no predetermined seating arrangements, no suggestion that these matters should be the sole responsibility of the teacher. The children decided the physical layout of the class: Loose seating groups dependent on what they would be doing; a quiet corner with bean bags and headphones; standing desks, plants, soft lights and plenty of wall space to show off their work; a post-it box where they could share any anxieties or wishes with their teacher in all anonymity. They discussed having soft music playing as they came into class first thing in the morning, interestingly mainly classical, and this became the precursor of circle time where birthdays are celebrated, family events shared, the list of who would be doing what that day discussed and anything else the children wanted to talk about. It appears to be working to the advantage of all, both socially and academically, and the headteacher is keen to promote this approach across all stages.

Now this takes courage, determination and informed leadership by an unpromoted member of staff. Perhaps more so, it takes the willingness of the headteacher, the other members of staff, the teaching assistants and, let's not forget, the janitors.

Kris rarely chooses to go to the nurture group now. But he knows the door is always open for him.

There has been an increasing interest, over time, in upscaling the principles of nurture to the whole establishment level (Education Scotland, 2016). To support this agenda, in 2016 Education Scotland created a draft version of the self-evaluation framework – *Applying nurture as a whole school approach: A framework to support the self-evaluation of nurturing approaches in schools and early learning and childcare settings*.

Nurture groups are described as having a positive impact on closing the attainment gap in Scotland in 'Closing the attainment gap in Scottish education' (Sosu & Ellis, 2014). At the heart of nurture is a focus on wellbeing and relationships and a drive to support the growth and development of children and young people, many of whom come from areas of disadvantage and require additional targeted support to close the equity gap (Boxall, 2002). Marjorie Boxall first conceived of the idea of nurture groups as a way of targeting children and young people who had come from impoverished backgrounds and needed additional support to help them with the re-creation of missed early experiences. Nurture groups in Scotland continue to target support towards children and young people who demonstrate such needs, but a wider nurturing approach is also increasingly being promoted in many primary, secondary and early learning and childcare settings to support the needs of a wider group of children and young people.

> The emphasis within a nurture group is on emotional growth, focusing on offering broad-based experiences in an environment that promotes security, routines, clear boundaries and carefully planned, repetitive learning opportunities. The aim of the nurture group is to create the world of earliest childhood, build in the basic and essential learning experiences normally gained in the first three years of life and enable learners and young people to fully meet their potential in mainstream schools.
>
> (Boxall, 2002, p. 13)

Applying nurture as a whole school approach (ANWSA) was published by Education Scotland in 2016. It was a framework to support the self-evaluation of nurturing approaches in schools and early learning and childcare (ELC) settings.

The 2016 document stated that research on the impact of nurture groups suggests, *inter alia*, that they can increase pupil engagement and significantly reduce school exclusions and lower truancy. Significant gains in academic attainment were depicted for pupils attending nurture groups, evaluated by their pre and post scores on a baseline assessment. This was shown by a progress in metacognition skills as well as language and literacy skills. There was a dearth of evidence, however, indicating that the application of nurturing approaches from the group to the establishment level has similar positive effects:

> when educators model nurturing with an honest smile and a helping hand, with patience, respect, dignity, understanding and flexibility, and when educators embrace learning, it is more likely their students will act the same way toward others.
>
> (Haapanen, 2014, p. 7)

Surely this is values in action.

Definition of a whole-school nurturing approach

Nolan et al. (2021) in a systematic review show how whole-school approaches emphasise the following:

1. A positive role model from teachers;
2. Positive relationships in school that are reliable, predictable and consistent;
3. Inclusive, respectful relationships across the whole school community, including learners, staff and parents/carers;
4. An understanding of attachment theory;
5. A balance of care and challenge;
6. Incorporation of attunement, warmth and connection;
7. Alongside structure, high expectations and a focus on achievement and attainment;
8. A particular focus on those pupils with missing early nurturing experiences;
9. The development of resilience and capacity to deal more confidently with life.

Features of a nurturing school

In Scotland, we have the acronym SHANARRI, which stands for the need for all children to be safe, healthy, achieving, nurtured, active, responsible, respected and included. Given the number of immigrant children attending school, we would add communication to SHANARRI.

Nolan et al. cite both Doyle (2003) and Lucas (1999), who describe the features of a nurturing school. Lucas (1999) emphasises the importance of a whole-school nurturing curriculum where relationships are key. It is suggested that education for personal relationships should be taught explicitly and pupils be actively involved in their learning and the curriculum interpreted developmentally. Having clear aims and objectives and clear school systems were part of the nurturing school (Doyle, 2003; Lucas, 1999), shared with all staff and pupils and publicised in all school documents.

In a nurturing school, the senior management team should have a clear system for behaviour management aligned to the nurturing approach (Nolan et al., 2021). In a nurturing school the senior management team should also view the school organically, have clear lines of delegation and accountability, and ensure all pupils and staff have the opportunity to express their views. A nurturing school will have systems in place for induction of new pupils, families and school staff and for parental involvement. Similarly, Doyle (2003) describes clear playtime and lunchtime routines. These include a smaller lunchtime environment facilitated by an adult for pupils who are overwhelmed by the unstructured playground; teaching children playground games during PE; and rewards for good manners and helping others (Nolan et al., 2021).

Inclusion is described as a feature of the nurturing school. Lucas (1999) advocated an inclusive approach to additional support needs, and Doyle (2003) suggested that a pastoral role be undertaken by all school staff. Doyle (2003) places emphasis on the importance of nurture group staff promoting their work in the wider school and mainstream staff getting the opportunity to do observation in the group. Physical changes to the classroom should include attractive areas for children to go to in order to develop feelings of security (Doyle, 2003).

Many of these features, say Nolan et al. (2021), could be seen as features that any school might have. Perhaps it is not so much a question of what principles underpin the school's ethos and development but the degree to which they are developed and espoused.

Burns et al. (2018) undertook an evaluation of a whole-school nurturing initiative in Scotland. They cite Ireson and Hallam (2005), who argue that pupils who feel supported within the school community are more likely to be intrinsically motivated and to become autonomous learners, thereby increasing the chances of positive pupil outcomes. Longitudinal research (Patrick et al., 2007; Wang & Holcombe, 2010) strengthens this view, as it found pupils' perceptions of the learning environment shaped their level of school participation and engagement the following academic year, consequently influencing their academic attainment.

Burns et al. (2018) concluded that their findings appear to highlight that schools' efforts to embed nurturing approaches are effectively contributing to a more positive and supportive environment for pupils in school, including those facing poverty-related educational barriers. This is extremely encouraging given that the literature has consistently demonstrated that a positive perception of learning environment increases a pupil's sense of belonging to a school.

Nurturing creativity

Thinking of nurturing ideas in education implies a need for careful thought and continued attention. Here, to illustrate nurturing, we use the example of creativity, as this, we suggest, always requires a degree of nurturing. We draw on the work of Collard and Looney (2014), where creativity is widely acknowledged as vital for social and economic innovation and development as well as for individual wellbeing. On a personal level, it is about the desire for self-expression and identity. Collard and Looney (2014) cite Martha Nussbaum (2011), who argues that human dignity and progress are rooted in each individual's capabilities, including those that are central to creativity: Being able to use the senses, imagine, think and reason, and to have the educational opportunities necessary to realise these capacities.

Collard and Looney refer to open and closed learning. 'Closed' learning refers to learning where the knowledge to be acquired is already well defined and goals are clear. 'Open' learning refers to learning where the outcome is unknown. Clearly nurturing creativity may be linked to both open and closed learning, where creativity is in the curriculum but with little guidance on what this means and how it should be approached with a class. Nurturing dispositions for creativity are described by Collard and Looney (2014). This includes nurturing characteristics of personality such as openness to experiences, curiosity, willingness to explore and ability to tolerate ambiguity. We would add ability to problem solve. They also cite sophisticated capabilities, such as effort and persistence, the ability to reflect critically and also synthesise ideas from diverse sources. Furthermore, they mention creative self-efficacy or a belief in one's capacity to address challenge and to persist.

For learners, the classroom and home environments, as well as the broader and social and cultural context, have a clear impact. Amabile (1990) noted that individuals were more creative in environments that encouraged exploration and independent work and that valued originality – in other words, in settings that encourage open learning. In turn, teachers are also more likely to focus on learner creativity and teaching creatively in school and policy environments that value and support them and encourage innovation and associated risks, and also allow them to develop their own creative dispositions.

Learning points

1. Nurturing is often associated with very young children, but we believe it is relevant to the education of all ages, including adults.
2. Of foremost importance is placing the child as a priority and nurturing positive child-teacher relationships, which are central to learning and wellbeing.
3. Children actively construct meaning in relation to their world through play and creativity.

Challenge questions

1. What does the term 'nurturing' mean to you? Do you think this is the role of primary school teachers?

2. Of the schools with which you are familiar, is there any nurturing, and if so in what ways? If not, is the impact on the child positive or negative?
3. Creativity is important to children, in our opinion. In what ways do you stimulate creativity in the classroom? Are you yourself creative with curriculum?

References

Amabile, T. M. (1990). Within you, without you: the social psychology of creativity, and beyond. In M.A. Runco & R.S. Albert (Eds.), *Theories of creativity* (Rev. ed.). Hampton Press, Cresskill, New Jersey, USA.

Bennathan, M., & Boxall, M. (2000). *Effective intervention in primary schools: Nurture groups* (2nd ed.). David Fulton, London.

Boxall, M. (2002). *Nurture groups in schools: Principles and practice.* SAGE, London.

Burns, J., MacDonald, A., & Ferguson, N. (2018). Improving pupils' perceptions of the learning environment through enhanced nurturing approaches: An evaluation. *The International Journal of Nurture in Education,* 4, 32-44.

Collard, P., & Looney, J. (2014). Nurturing creativity in education. *European Journal of Education,* 49(3). https://doi.org/10.1111/ejed.12090

Doyle, R. (2003). Developing the nurturing school: Spreading nurture group principles and practices into mainstream classrooms. *Emotional and Behavioural Difficulties,* 8(4), 252-266.

Education Scotland. (2016). *Applying nurture as a whole school approach (ANWSA): A framework to support the self-evaluation of nurturing approaches in schools and early learning and childcare (ELC) settings.* Education Scotland, Livingston, Scotland, UK.

Haapanen, I. (2014). Nurture and change: The establishment of a dynamic and responsive teacher education classroom. *Policy Futures in Education,* 12(6). www.wwwords.co.uk/PFIE)

Hayes, N., & Filipović, K. (2018). Nurturing 'buds of development': From outcomes to opportunities in early childhood practice. *International Journal of Early Years Education,* 26(3), 220-232. https://doi.org/10.1080/09669760.2017.1341303

Ireson, J., & Hallam, S. (2005). Pupils' liking for school: Ability grouping, self-concept and perceptions of teaching. *British Journal of Educational Psychology.* https://doi.org/10.1348/000709904X24762

Lucas, S. (1999). The nurturing school: The impact of nurture group principles and practice on the whole school. *Emotional and Behavioural Difficulties,* 4(3), 14-19.

McNicol, S., & Reilly, L. (2015). Applying nurture as a whole school approach. *Educational & Child Psychology,* 35(3), 44-59.

Morris, J. (2018). *Children's construction of their experiences in a primary school nurture group.* Thesis submitted for the degree of doctor of education at the University of Leicester, England, UK.

Noddings, N. (1984). *Caring: A feminine approach to ethics and moral education.* University of California Press, Berkeley.

Nolan, A.D., Hannah, E.F.S., Lakin, E., & Topping, K.J. (2021). Whole-school nurturing approaches: A systematic analysis of impact. *Educational and Child Psychology,* 38(1), 10-23.

Nussbaum, M. (2011). *Creating capabilities: The human development approach.* Harvard University Press, Cambridge, MA.

OECD. (n.d.). *The case for 21st-century learning.* https://www.bollettinoadapt.it/old/files/document/11702schleicher_oecd_.pdf

Patrick, H., Ryan, A.M., & Kaplan, A. (2007). Early adolescents' perceptions of the classroom social environment, motivational beliefs, and engagement. *Journal of Educational Psychology,* 99(1), 83-98. https://doi.org/10.1037/0022-0663.99.1.83

Sosu, E., & Ellis, S. (2014). *Closing the attainment gap in Scottish education.* Joseph Rowntree Foundation, York, Yorkshire, UK.

Wang, M., & Holcombe, R., (2010). Adolescents' perceptions of school environment, engagement, and academic achievement in middle school. *American Educational Research Journal,* 47(3), 633-662.

12 Leadership

Leadership and leadership practice

Over the last few decades, research into leadership has moved away from hero worshipping 'great leaders' to promoting leadership styles, with transformative and instructional leadership gaining most traction in educational circles. John Hattie (2023, p. 174) distinguished between 'instructional' and 'transformation' notions of leadership, but these terms are becoming so muddled that it may be time to move past them. This is certainly the case in educational leadership research.

> Despite several decades of research on theoretically-derived leadership styles, there is still no consensus about their relative impacts on student outcomes. That may be why educational leadership researchers are increasingly studying the impact of leadership practices.
>
> (Robinson & Gray, 2019, p. 174)

Leadership practice asks not what we need to be to become a leader but what we need to do. Accordingly, General Teaching Council Scotland defines leadership as the ability to:

- Develop a vision for change, which leads to improvements in outcomes for learners and is based on shared values and robust evaluation of evidence of current practice and outcomes;
- Mobilise, enable and support others to develop and follow through on strategies for achieving that change.

(GTC Scotland, 2021, The Standard for Middle Leadership, p. 6)

We agree with Spillane (2013) that 'Equating leadership solely with the actions of those in formal leadership positions is inadequate as leadership involves many leaders, some with, and some without, formal leadership positions: It is not the actions of individuals, but the interactions among them, that are critical in leadership practice.' Harris explains further, 'the vast literature on educational change reinforces, again and again, the centrality of teacher agency, collaboration and leadership as a core influence upon improved learner outcomes' (Harris and Jones, 2019, p. 123).

Teachers should, we propose, recognise and value their own roles as leaders of learning in their classroom, across school and beyond. We need to move away from seeing the leader as a certain type of person; rather we are all leaders who need to reflect and develop our practice to create a culture of leaders within the educational environments in which we work.

Leadership in teachers' professional standards across the UK

Around the world every country will have its own professional standards to which teachers are held accountable. In Scotland, the standards expect all teachers to be leaders of and for learning:

> The professional commitment of teachers in Scotland is to lead learning through:
>
> - developing deep knowledge of learning and teaching;
> - critically examining how our teaching impacts on learners;
> - using evidence collaboratively to inform teacher judgement and next steps for learners.
>
> (GTCS, 2021, Standards for Full Registration, p. 5)

These leadership practices stop short of expecting leadership across the school community, and it is only if the teacher chooses to follow the standards for career-long professional learning that there is an expectation to lead on and have critical understanding of leadership practices for curriculum development.

Despite half of teachers in England (DFE, 2023a, Working Lives of Teachers and Leaders – Year 1, p. 22) taking on teaching and learning responsibility (TLR) payments, which reward taking on additional leadership and management duties alongside normal classroom delivery, the Department for Education Teaching Standards do not mention leadership. TLRs often mean taking leadership of a curriculum area, pupil development or a stand-alone project. Encouragingly, since 2021, there have been government-funded national professional qualifications in leading specific areas to support teacher professional development.

In contrast, in Wales, leadership is explicitly identified as one of the five standards of the expectations of a professional teacher. The leadership standards expect that 'the teacher exercises leadership through all aspects of professional practice to support the efforts of others across the school and beyond to fulfil the educational ambitions for Wales' (Welsh Government, 2019, Professional Standards for Teaching and Leadership, p. 56).

In Northern Ireland, the standards set out the teacher competencies which includes the vision that 'Every teacher is a learning leader, accomplished in working collaboratively with all partners in the interests of children and young people' (Department of Education, 2016, p. 4).

Overall, it is encouraging that professional bodies are increasingly recognising the importance of leadership across all levels of teaching.

Leadership practices

In the next section we shall consider what are good leadership practices. In 2008, Leithwood, Harris and Hopkins published the influential 'Seven Strong Claims of Successful School Leadership,' arguing that almost all successful school leaders draw on the same repertoire of leadership practices within four domains of practice:

- Building vision and setting directions;
- Building relationships and developing people;
- Developing the organization to support desired practices;
- Improving the instructional program.

(Leithwood et al., 2008, p. 29)

They claimed that leadership has most influence when it is distributed widely (Leithwood, Harris and Hopkins, 2019). In other words, teachers at all levels have a duty to consider these leadership practices for a school to be successful.

In this next section we will consider the four domains and the leadership practises identified by Leithwood et al. (2008, 2019) and discuss how they can help leaders at all levels, including classroom teachers.

Leadership domain 1: Building vision and setting directions

Leadership practices include the following:

- Build a shared vision;
- Identify specific, shared, short-term goals;
- Create high-performance expectations;
- Communicate the vision and goals.

Building a shared vision is a powerful statement of intent and when done effectively will encompass the values and aspirations of the whole school community. John recently worked with the whole school community, including children, their families, teaching and support staff, to review the vision of the school in which he works. He asked the question, 'After you have read the vision, would this be a school in which you'd be enthusiastic to work?' The vision is not the responsibility of the school's head teacher, it should be built together and should motivate every member of the school community: staff, pupils and parents; to want to bring it to realisation over time. It should guide key decision making throughout the school. For example, if you decide you want your school or classroom to be inclusive, any decisions around environments, structures and communication should have inclusion at the forefront of the process, and any compromises should be reduced to a minimum.

A shared vision also means that goals are more likely to be achieved collectively. Robinson writes 'effective goal setting, requires gaining commitment of all those involved by linking goals to values which people hold dearly; ensuring that staff have or can acquire the capabilities needed to achieve the goals, and using evidence about current levels of student achievement to set important and realistic targets' (Robinson, 2025).

This is as true in the staffroom as it is in the classroom. Shirley Clarke, who has written many books on formative assessment and goal setting in education, explains, 'The foundation [of good formative assessment and goal setting] is that there is a learning culture, where pupils have self-efficacy and know how to learn, and teachers have high expectations and a belief that all pupils can succeed (TES, 2025).

Our role as leaders is not only to ensure our pupils and staff want to change but, importantly, have the capabilities to meet their goals and have confidence in their belief that they can achieve it.

Leadership domain 2: Building relationships and developing people

Leadership practices include the following:

- Provide support and demonstrate consideration for individuals;
- Model the school's values and practices;
- Build trusting relationships with and among staff, students and parents;
- Establish productive working relationships with teacher federation representatives.

At all levels, our most important job as leaders is to build relationships. Encouragingly, a Pearson survey into the top qualities of a teacher in England, 'the ability to develop trusting, productive relationships' came out top (Pearson Education, 2025). Relationships need to be both authentic and mutual.

In his book *Dusting Off the Thunderbolts*, ex-headteacher and leadership speaker Sir John Jones (2023) rightly raises concerns about 'the plethora of leadership books that imply leadership is simply a case of learning how to play the notes' (p. 13). He goes on to explain leadership has 'deep humanity at its core' (p. 14), quoting a saying: "People forget what you said, people forget what you did but people will never forget how you made them feel" (p. 14).

As good teachers, we should believe our pupils learn best when we share a relationship built on trust and respect. Pupils should know the teacher has genuine interest in them, wants to do the right thing for them and wants to develop their capacity to learn and grow. Wellbeing was discussed in Chapter 10.

For some teachers, building relationships might feel like an unrealistic expectation, for example, 'for the Religious Education teacher who has 340 pupils for half an hour once every two weeks' (Dix, 2017, p. 37). Dix further explains that relationships do not mean 'dramatic displays of affection or wanting your personal life poured out… but the small stuff, the daily acts of care, the perpetual generosity of spirit, the interest you show in their lives that matters most. … The act of being bothered' (Dix, 2017, p. 38). A good leader at all levels understands you need to be 'bothered' about those in your community. An example of a teacher being 'bothered' and the empowerment this created can be found in Chapter 5, Kindness.

Leadership domain 3: Developing the organization to support desired practices

Leadership practices include the following:

- Build collaborative culture and distribute leadership;
- Structure the organization to facilitate collaboration;
- Build productive relationships with families and communities;
- Connect the school to its wider environment;
- Maintain a safe and healthy school environment;
- Allocate resources in support of the school's vision and goals.

It is recognised that leadership has an effect if widely distributed (Leithwood et al., 2019). 'Distributed leadership implies a model of shared, collective, and extended leadership practice where the emphasis is upon interdependent interactions rather than individual and independent actions' (Harris et al., 2022, p. 439). What is important is how these interdependent interactions are organised and supported.

When formal leaders provide opportunities for shared leadership by affording others the power to make decisions, everyone benefits (Donohoo, 2017). 'Teachers are empowered when they have a voice in school decisions' (Donohoo, 2017, p. 40). She argues that to achieve this, collective efficacy is required.

Collective efficacy is creating a genuine belief that all children can succeed, regardless of background. This doesn't mean we discount background; far from it. We need be very aware of the socioeconomic and cultural backgrounds of our pupils, but we are determined to not allow this to stop any learner from succeeding. It has been identified as having the greatest impact on student achievement (Hattie, 2023). Tschannen-Moran and Barr (2004) define it as a 'collective self- perception that teachers in a given school make an educational difference to their students over and above the educational impact of their homes and communities' (p. 190, as cited in Donohoo, 2017, p. 1).

The leadership practices required for collective efficacy complement those already identified, such as goal setting, creating meaningful collaboration, empowering teachers and helping teams interpret results and feedback (Donohoo, 2017), meaning that 'collaboration has positive effects on teaching and learning' (Hattie, 2023, p. 228). Well planned collaboration can empower teachers, reduce workload (DFE, 2023b) and benefit the whole school. This can have a positive impact on student outcomes as improvements are made by motivated teachers.

Penny reflected on a time when she had a successful, meaningful collaboration:

> I participated in an Education Empowerment Fund pilot project at school, which aimed to improve pupils' attitude to learning and use strategies such as metacognition, self-regulation and feedback. Collaboration with chosen staff in school was key to the success of the project, which proved difficult at first. However, once the project was refined, with only two teachers and clear outcomes, collaboration became much easier, with clear goals and a set timetable. The main outcomes were successful, with an increase in the proportion of teachers who were positively disposed to academic research to inform their own teaching practice.

However, collaboration has its pitfalls, as Donohoo (2017) explains. Collaborative groups can fall into groupthink, with groups becoming polarized, sharing information they already know or following the first speaker (DFE, 2023b). Groups can also be at risk of members trying to dominate the discourse and belittle others who they disagree with. It may be the formal leader's role to monitor this, but this is not always easy as Karen found when leading an educational project.

> Karen was director of an educational project which required expert outside support in information technology. Karen became aware that the expert and a staff member, who was project co-ordinator, were not getting on well. There was a hint of verbal bullying between the expert, Peter, and the project co-ordinator, Amy. A power game from the expert about who was cleverest was taking place. This made Amy unhappy and

self-critical of everything she did. As the leader, Karen was best placed to sort this out, but she did not act immediately, because the project deadline needed the expert. As it happened, other staff from the project solved the problem by acting quickly and talking to Peter. They also worked together to solve the IT problems themselves.

Karen feels she should have acted more quickly and the project was not as important as Amy's feelings. Sometimes, when you are very busy and under pressure it is easy, as a leader, to lose sight of what matters.

It's not just about teacher voice. We need to recognise the importance of pupil voice as a right, not a privilege. As a leader of learning we have a responsibility to foster this within our classrooms. A Scottish study has shown that schools located in areas of deprivation that achieve better-than-expected exam results were all making comprehensive efforts to address learner participation across school life (Mannion et al., 2015). Furthermore, where pupils are actively involved in contributing to discussions and decisions about teaching and learning, they develop a deeper understanding of learning processes, which promotes the development of higher order thinking skills (Flutter & Rudduck, 2004).

In the Curriculum for Wales Framework, schools are given the opportunity to design their own curriculum, building their own vision within the context of the four purposes and the learning defined at a national level. As schools develop their vision to support their learners to realise the four purposes, learner voices are fully expected be central to this.

Maintaining orderly and safe environments

Robinson and Gray (2019) argue that ensuring an orderly and safe environment is one of the key dimensions to successful leadership. We agree that it is important to spend time considering the physical environment, As Brighouse (2007) suggests making sure the classroom teaching and learning materials are well-organised and in plentiful supply improving the staffroom and the whole environment of school visually and aurally (p. 10). Robinson (2011, p. 125) explains, 'If students and staff do not feel physically and psychologically safe, if discipline codes are perceived as unfair and inconsistently enforced, then little progress is likely in the improvement of teaching and learning.' Classroom management has been discussed in Chapter 5, Kindness, and Chapter 8, Tolerance and Patience.

Environments are of paramount importance to pupils with additional support needs. Scotland has produced the Circle Framework, which supports teachers to set up an inclusive environment for all students by considering the physical and social environment and the classroom structures and routines (Circle Framework, 2021).

Leadership domain 4: Improving the instructional program

Leadership practices include the following:

- Staff the instructional program;
- Provide instructional support;
- Monitor student learning and school improvement progress;
- Buffer staff from distractions to their instructional work.

Curriculums evolve. Scotland has recently launched a decade-long review of the Curriculum for Excellence following advice from the OECD. As good leaders, we need to be able to understand if change is really happening. Many English primary teachers will be given the additional role of subject lead and may want to improve their curriculum area, giving it prominence in the school improvement plan. However, we need to take care, as too many initiatives can lead to these not being given the time needed or even contribute to staff burnout. It is important as leaders that we consider the pace of change.

When a new development is in place, it is important to allocate time to interpret results and provide feedback. This requires robust and reliable data and the ability to analyse and interpret the results. Interpreting results, by examining student learning data, helps strengthen connections between the learning task, content, instruction and student outcomes (Donohoo, 2017). We must also consider that new developments can also raise concerns amongst teachers that the process will surface questions related to professional expertise.

Leaders are themselves good learners who understand that we can always improve and that we can always be better. Jones (2023) recalls a time when he met a teacher called Bill. At the end of the day, Bill took 15 minutes for what he called reflection time.

> John Dewey, the old sage, said that you do not learn from experience, you learn by reflecting on experience. So, you can ask yourself three questions: What have I done today that was brilliant and I want to share? What have I done that I never want to repeat? and How will this learning affect my tomorrow?
>
> (Jones, 2023, p. 72)

Effective continuing professional development is likely to consist of that which first and foremost enhances pupil outcomes but which also helps to bring about changes in practice and improves teaching (Bubb & Earley, 2007).

Learning points

1. Leadership is not necessarily about who the person is but more importantly what the person does.
2. Qualities like resilience and charisma are certainly useful and may help a leader get through certain situations, but unless the leader is choosing their leadership practices carefully the change needed may not come to fruition.
3. Teachers must consider themselves leaders and must allocate time to consider the actions they take to enable positive change, both within their classroom and throughout the school.
4. Working uncompromisingly to achieve the school vision, setting realistic and achievable goals, thinking deeply about pedagogy, building relationships, trusting others and accepting the reality of the results provided by robust and rigorous data are all actions a leader must practice at all levels.

Challenge Questions

1. Do you consider yourself to be a leader?
2. How do you communicate and realise the school vision both within your classroom and across the school?
3. How do you ensure pupil voice is central to goal setting?
4. Have you had any meaningful collaboration? Reflect on whether it was successful or not and why that might be the case.
5. When have you realised you may be taking the wrong direction? How did you address this?

References

Brighouse, T. (2007). How head teachers survive and thrive. https://www.rm.com/-/media/PDFs/Clean-Sheet/2023/Sir-Tim-Brighouse/How_head_teachers_survive_and_thrive_by_prof_tim_brighouse.pdf?la=en&hash=8434A8EE246BFADA5E4F65F72D5CCDF2CA7D28C6

Bubb, S., & Earley, P. (2007). *Leading and managing continuing professional development* (2nd ed). Paul Chapman, London.

Circle Framework. (2021). Primary CIRCLE resource 2021. https://www.thirdspace.scot/wp-content/uploads/2021/01/Primary-CIRCLE-Resource-2021.pdf

Department of Education. (2016). *Learning leaders: A strategy for teacher professional learning*. Bangor, Northern Ireland.

Department for Education. (2023a). *Working lives of teachers and leaders -Year 1: Government Social Research*.

Department for Education. (2023b). *Exploring school collaboration and workload reduction*. Government Social Research.

Dix, P. (2017). *When adults change everything changes*. Independent Thinking Press, Carmarthen, Wales.

Donohoo, J. (2017). *Collective efficacy: How educators' beliefs impact student learning*. Corwin, Thousand Oaks, CA.

Flutter, J., & Rudduck, J. (2004). *Consulting pupils: What's in it for schools?* Routledge, London.

General Teaching Council (GTCS). (2021). *The standard for middle leadership*. Edinburgh, Scotland

General Teaching Council Scotland. (2021). *The standard for full registration*. Edinburgh, Scotland.

Harris, A., & Jones, M. (2019). Teacher leadership and educational change. *School Leadership & Management*, 39(2), 123-126.

Harris, A., Jones, M., & Ismail, N. (2022). Distributed leadership: Taking a retrospective and contemporary view of the evidence base. *School Leadership & Management*, 42(5), 438-456.

Hattie, J. (2023). *Visible learning: The sequel*. Routledge, Abingdon, Oxon, UK.

Jones, J. (2023). *Dusting off thunderbolts: A quest for the heart of leadership*. John Catt Educational Hodder Education, Woodbridge, Suffolk.

Leithwood, K., Harris, A., & Hopkins, D. (2008). Seven strong claims about successful school leadership. *School Leadership & Management*, 28(1), 27-42.

Leithwood, K., Harris, A., & Hopkins, D. (2019). Seven strong claims about successful school leadership revisited. *School Leadership & Management*, 40(1), 5-22.

Mannion, G., Sowerby, M., & I'Anson, J. (2015). *How young people's participation in school supports achievement and attainment*. Children and Young People's Commissioner Scotland, Edinburgh.

Pearson Education. (2025). England: What makes an effective teacher. https://www.pearson.com/content/dam/corporate/global/pearson-dot-com/files/innovation/global-survey/reports/RINVN9283_UK_July_090516.pdf

Robinson, V. (2011). *Student centred leadership*. Jossey-Bass, London.

Robinson, V. (2025). Leadership where it counts. *Teaching Times*. www.teachingtimes.com/leadership-where-it-counts/?download_file=1

Robinson, V., & Gray, E. (2019). What difference does school leadership make to student outcomes? *Journal of the Royal Society of New Zealand*, 49(2), 171-187.

Spillane, J. (2013). The practice of leading and managing teaching in educational organisations. In *Leadership for 21st century learning, Centre for Educational Research and Innovation*. OECD Publishing, Paris, pp. 60–77.

Times Educational Supplement. (2025). Shirley Clarke: Formative assessment has lost its way. https://www.tes.com/magazine/teaching-learning/general/shirley-clarke-interview-formative-assessment

Tschannen-Moran, M., & Barr, M. (2004). Fostering student learning: The relationship of collective teacher efficacy and student achievement. *Leadership and Policy in Schools*, 3(3), 189–209.

Welsh Government. (2019). *Professional standards for teaching and leadership*. https://hwb.gov.wales/storage/19bc948b-8a3f-41e0-944a-7bf2cadf7d18/professional-standards-for-teaching-and-leadership-interactive-pdf-for-pc.pdf

13 Knowledge

We hope you will view professional learning as an adventure and, also, as self-awareness.

Introduction

'Knowledge' and 'knowing' are both difficult terms according to Scheffler (1999). Knowing is closely related to notions of understanding and ideas of contemplation, absorption and appreciation. Knowledge is not simply descriptive; it expresses *inter alia* our standards, our ideas and our tastes. The mind can do many things with knowledge; it can compare, combine, analyse and generalise upon materials furnished to it by experience (Scheffler, 1999). How we use and interpret knowledge as educators is linked inevitably to our values and beliefs.

Radical constructivism is an idea that human beings build up knowledge in a slow process, with simple sensory knowledge at first and more complex ideas as the individual gets older. Social constructivism looks at people differently. Vygotsky (1978) regards knowledge as being an interplay between nature and history, biology and culture. Vygotsky (1978) sees robust understanding and knowledge to be socially constructed through collaborative talk and interaction in and around activities (Roth, 1999). Situated cognition suggests thinking cannot be understood as apart from the contexts in which it appears. Thus, thinking as well as knowing and remembering are thought to be distributed rather than residing in the head of an individual.

Teacher knowledge can be thought of as one facet of competence and can further be subdivided into different subsets. In a seminal work, Shulman (1986) identified three content-related facets and one generic facet, namely content knowledge, pedagogical content knowledge, curricular knowledge and general pedagogical knowledge. A teacher needs to develop all four of these to be able to deal effectively with the various challenges of her job. Blömeke et al. (2014), describing mathematics education, demonstrate just some of the complexity of managing knowledge in practice:

Lesson planning knowledge is essential before mathematics instruction in the classroom can begin. The mathematics content must be selected appropriately, simplified and connected to teaching strategies taking into account possible learning difficulties or learning barriers caused by, inter alia, misconceptions of central mathematical concepts and methods. Knowledge about the way in which students learn should be taken into account when selecting a teaching strategy as well. Such knowledge requires teachers in turn to review students' answers, verbal or written, in the context of the tasks or questions given to them. Teachers should ask questions of varying complexity, identify misconceptions, provide feedback and react with appropriate scaffolding or intervention strategies. Teachers have to consider curricular issues such as the order of topics in primary or lower-secondary curriculum and need to develop their lesson planning in accordance with curricular requirements. Pedagogical content knowledge may depend on the teaching and learning philosophy of the pedagogical context a teacher is working in and other cultural influences such as differences between Eastern and Western educational traditions.

(Blömeke et al., 2014)

We consider this list to be by no means complete. The processes of teaching a subject are multiple and demand knowledge from a wide range of levels and from different disciplines. The teacher needs to synthesise these multiple processes into a hopefully harmonious experience for the children.

Hierarchies of knowledge

We know things in many different ways. See the following incomplete list. Different ways of knowing are valued in different ways by the general public and by us as educators. Some have more prestige or importance than others, and some are valued more highly than others. Numbers generally make the knowing to be perceived as more important.

We can know, *inter alia*, through:

- Cognition, problem solving, and reasoning;
- Authority;
- Experience, practice, touch, or smell;
- Emotion;
- Aesthetics;
- Imagination;
- Ethics;
- Intuition;
- Spirituality;
- History and tradition;
- Common sense;

- Interrelationships (e.g., authority/experience);
- Research.

Thinking of the power that resides in knowledge and knowing, Young (1999) asks, what is the scope of the curriculum provided for different groups, and what factors influence this? Young (1999) goes on to say all curricula involve assumptions that some kinds and areas of knowledge are more worthwhile than others. Currently, you simply have to think about the relative importance of maths and music in the curriculum to see the differences in valuing taught subjects. Maths appears to be more valued by decision makers than music, in terms of time given to it in the curriculum.

Knowledge of content for teaching

Ben-Peretz (2011) describes how teachers do not only need content knowledge of a curriculum but also the wider subject knowledge, which includes an understanding of the various ways a discipline can be organized or understood, as well as the knowledge of the ways by which a discipline evaluates and accepts new knowledge. Yet this complex understanding of subject matter is not conceived to be enough for teachers. What is needed is a specialized body of knowledge, namely pedagogical content knowledge.

Occasionally, Ben-Peretz suggests in reporting on research about knowing, that when prospective teachers won mastery of a subject at university, at first it blinded them to potential student difficulties. Actual contact with students forced these teachers to re-examine their subject matter content from a new perspective. They learned to evaluate their subject matter from the perspective of children. Teachers' knowledge base, as far as subject matter knowledge is concerned, has to include opportunities for re-examining subject matter content from the perspective of student learning – in Shulman's (1986) terms, 'pedagogic content knowledge.' So, within subject knowledge you need to know the curriculum, how people learn, and different learning strategies for different children. In short, you need pedagogical knowledge. You also need self-awareness and reflexivity (see Chapters 1 and 3) to be clear to yourself about what makes you choose particular content over others. Are you placing knowledge in a hierarchy?

Recently, discussions around content and subject matter have focused on technology and mathematics. We take technology education as a case in point to discuss subject knowledge with an example. Rohaan et al. (2012) discuss the fact that when high-quality technology education is aimed for, high-quality technology teachers are required. But what do primary school teachers need to know, they ask, to become high-quality technology teachers? And what are the cognitions and beliefs that underlie teachers' behaviour during technology activities?

They recommended that teacher education should first focus on the development of teachers' subject matter knowledge and pedagogical content knowledge. This knowledge will positively affect teachers' confidence in teaching and, in turn, their attitude towards the subject. More confidence in technology teaching and a more positive attitude are expected to increase the frequency of technology education, which consequently increases teaching experience and thereby stimulates the development of teachers' pedagogical content knowledge.

This circle of positive reinforcement will eventually contribute, Rohaan et al. (2012) suggest, to the quality of technology education. Furthermore, teacher knowledge is integrated knowledge, consisting of scientific as well as non-scientific elements. Beliefs are closely interwoven and play an important role in constructing and organising teacher knowledge.

Rohaan et al. (2012) also explain how teachers should become familiar with pedagogical approaches that are suitable for technology education, such as inquiry-based and problem-based learning. Moreover, they should be made aware of the nature, purpose and characteristics of technology education. This implies, say Rohaan et al. (2012), that they should learn to ask provoking questions, use powerful analogies, explain the subject matter in various ways and recognise common misconceptions. Most time should be spent on hands-on technology activities ('teach what you preach').

Actually doing and experiencing technology education is expected to increase teachers' confidence in teaching technology most effectively themselves. In the end, more profound knowledge of teaching technology will help teachers to recognise the added value of high-quality technology education.

Now we take maths as our second case in point and Walshaw's (2012) thinking about teacher knowledge. Sound content knowledge is a prerequisite for accessing students' conceptual understandings and for deciding where these understandings might be heading. It plays a critical role in extending and challenging children's conceptual ideas. Sound subject knowledge enables teachers to mediate between the mathematical tasks, the artefacts, the talk and the actions surrounding teaching/learning encounters. Teachers with limited subject knowledge, Walshaw (2012) suggests, have been shown to focus on a narrow conceptual field rather than on forging wider connections between the facts, concepts, structures and practices of mathematics.

Pedagogical content knowledge influences the connections teachers make between aspects of mathematical knowledge. It also influences the interactions between the teacher and students as well as the teacher's professional reflections-in-action within the classroom. In short, sound content and pedagogical content knowledge provides the resources for an on-the-spot synthesis of actions, thinking, theories and principles within classroom interactions.

Thinking now about literacy, Adoniou (2014), from a broad literature review, identified the following six knowledge domains as being important to teacher knowledge. While these knowledge domains could be applied to any teaching, descriptions are provided for how they apply specifically to literacy teaching.

1. **Knowledge about content**: Specifically, understanding how the English language works in literacy and literature.
2. **Knowledge about theory**: Theoretical understandings about teaching literacy, and their history.
3. **Knowledge about teaching**: Pedagogical understandings of how to teach literacy. This could also be described through Shulman's (1986) notion of pedagogical content knowledge; the capacity of teachers to apply their general pedagogic skills to teach discipline content (Shulman, 1986), including the curriculum documents they must work with, in order to plan and assess.

4. **Knowledge about their learners**: The literacy learning needs of the diversity of children in the teachers' classrooms.
5. **Knowledge about school context**: The school and community they teach in and how these may impact upon the literacy teaching strategies they require and the ways in which they are required to plan, report, assess and administer their literacy teaching.
6. **Knowledge about the sociocultural politics of teaching**: The ways in which larger political agendas impact upon the teaching of literacy, for example, national testing or school league tables.

(Adoniou, 2014, p. 101)

Adoniou (2014) explains that in the area of literacy education, the Australian government some time ago mandated what constitutes 'content' in literacy teaching, with the development of the Australian Curriculum for subject English (ACARA, 2012). For subject English, content descriptors were organised under three interrelated strands: language, literature and literacy. Thus, in the subject English, teachers must have a content knowledge of how the English language works (linguistic knowledge), how English literature is constructed (literary knowledge) and how communication happens in English (literacy knowledge). Three key, interrelated elements are identified: an explicit knowledge about language, an informed appreciation of literature and expanding repertoires of language use. Of these three, it is the language strand, and particularly the approach to grammar, that is arguably least understood (Derewianka, 2012).

Derewianka (2012) states that all students need to develop their understanding of how language functions to achieve a range of purposes that are critical to success in school. This includes reading, understanding, and writing texts that describe, narrate, analyse, explain, recount, argue, review and so on. Such an approach aims to:

- Extend students' language resources in ways that support increasingly complex learning throughout the school years;
- Help students deal with the language demands of the various curriculum areas;
- Enable students to move from the interactive spontaneity of oral language towards the denser, more crafted language of the written mode;
- Help students, in their speaking and writing, to move to and fro between the general and the specific, the abstract and the concrete, and the argument and the evidence;
- Raise students' awareness generally of interpersonal issues such as how to take and support a stand in an argument, how to express considered opinions, how to strengthen or soften statements, how to interact with a variety of audiences, and so on.

(ACARA, 2012, p. 10)

To capture the critical role of language envisaged in the curriculum requires a rich, robust model of language that is powerful enough to deal with all the demands made upon it. These include:

- Supporting students' learning from the early years through to late adolescence;
- Strengthening language and literacy development across the curriculum;
- Encompassing the basic skills as well as a focus on meaning;
- Operating at the levels of word, sentence and text and being able to explain how these are interrelated;
- Providing a basis for teaching and assessing oral interaction, reading, viewing and composing;
- Providing explicit assistance for students with specific language needs (e.g., EAL, Indigenous);
- Heightening the appreciation of literary texts;
- Contributing to a critical analysis of discourse;
- Fostering in students a curiosity about how language works.

(ACARA, 2012, p. 14)

In proposing such a central role for language, the new curriculum deliberately challenged teachers to re-imagine what a future-oriented discipline of English might look like (Derewianka, 2012). All the preceding bullet points show the inherent complexity associated with teaching a particular subject. Adoniou (2014) further explains that the consequences of a lack of content knowledge in teaching literacy can be serious, with Shulman (1986) indicating that lack of content knowledge results in narrowed and regressionist pedagogies, as teachers resort to replicating their own past experiences with instruction in language.

Teachers need to know a great deal, in many areas and in multiple ways, suggests Adoniou (2014). Teacher knowledge is a complex tapestry, and teachers must successfully weave the multiple threads, or otherwise risk 'getting lost in the cross-stitch.' To help conceptualise the complexity and thus identify the challenges, she has presented a framework through which to view teacher knowledge. The framework describes three ways of knowing: 'knowing how,' 'knowing why,' and 'knowing what,' and then applies these knowledge discourses across the six domains of teacher knowledge as presented earlier.

So far, we have discussed content knowledge. Now John provides a description of pedagogical content.

Pedagogical content knowledge

Have you ever said, would you like the 'bigger half?' or 'give me a wee minute,' and have you ever wondered why maths is confusing to some of our learners? It was as a new teacher that I attended a course run by a maths company, which changed the way I thought about maths teaching. The presenter asked us to consider the words we use and how these might be confusing for our young learners. For example, imagine a large number 3 drawn on a piece of paper and next to it a very small number 5. When we ask, 'which is the larger number?' you can understand the confusion caused. Another example: 'Today we are learning about take away.' Some children would instantly be thinking about take-away food and be confused or excited at the prospect of a bag of chips!

Subtraction was often highlighted as an area of development in our school; this made us all reflect on the words we use – terms like 'take away,' 'subtract,' or 'find the difference.' We might ask a pupil to find the difference between 8 and 12. The answers to a young learner might seem obvious: They look different. They may have an idea that difference is linked to subtraction, which is a 'take away sum.' They may then decide to take away 8 and 12 and try 8 – 12 and get confused when taking away on their hands and running out of fingers. The teacher will explain we are 'counting on' to find the answer. Adding to the confusion because they thought we were 'taking away,' but now you are saying that we are 'counting on' – is this not adding? The training went on to explain their approach was based on Bruner's model of learning; you learn first through doing, second through image representations and finally through language or abstract representations. Allowing children time to work through these stages is important, as it allows them to explore these misconceptions and support their understanding.

In my current role at a complex needs school, early language development and mathematics develop side by side and can lead to confusion and frustration. At the earliest stages, we begin to compare. As teachers, we want the learner to understand the concept of 'more' when comparing different amounts of objects; for example you have three teddies in one box, and I have four. We ask 'Who has more?'

However, this can lead to confusion as one of the first Makaton signs/words our learners develop is 'more,' often when they would like to 'have more,' such as 'more fruit,' or to continue to do an activity, that is 'do more.'' 'More' has different meanings depending on the context, not something our learners with complex learning needs and autism find easy to understand. It requires a skilled teacher to provide lots of experiences and interactions, through both play and real-life experiences, for our pupils to work through these concepts.

As teachers, our job isn't simply to impart knowledge, to fill the empty vessel, but to consider the misconceptions and connections that are likely to be encountered and to allow pupils to experience and understand these at the stage they are at. Having this pedagogical content knowledge cannot be overstated. Not considering this knowledge leads to significant barriers in later learning and learners sadly losing confidence in subjects in which they might have otherwise flourished.

The knowledgeable teacher

The last section showed the complexity associated with teaching a particular content. The teacher is indeed knowledgeable across multiple dimensions. Connelly et al. (1997) discuss what they term 'personal practical knowledge.' It is a term designed to capture the idea of experience in a way that allows us to talk about teachers as knowledgeable and knowing persons. They describe how the past, present and future are represented in teacher knowledge. Personal practical knowledge is in the teacher's past experience, in the teacher's present mind and body and in their future plans and actions. Personal practical knowledge is found in the teacher's practice. It is, for any one teacher, a particular way of reconstructing the past and the intentions of the future to deal with the exigencies of a present situation. They emphasise that teachers do not apply subject matter knowledge; they create their personal-practical knowledge of teaching.

Self-awareness

You will find that we discuss self-awareness quite frequently in this book, because it is so important to being a good teacher. Karen and Alison have explored self-awareness in a book chapter on professional knowledge (McArdle & Hurrell, 2016). Self-awareness is important so that we can be aware of our traits or qualities and how these contribute to, or impede, our professional practice. We do not, however, believe that a teacher's identity is fixed and can be discovered. It is rather, multiple and changing and needs to be consistently rediscovered, and there are multiple methods of doing this. We are of the view that courage and criticality are important to self-awareness.

Mead (2020) suggests that the key factor for educating teachers should be to nurture them as citizens who can exercise a dynamic relationship between personal moral decision making and political action in the classroom. Political action is linked to judgements about what matters in society and education. Mead further suggests that teachers' identity and autonomy are more likely to emerge when there is a dynamic relationship between personal moral and political values as citizens of a school. This kind of professional knowledge is further needed, suggests Mead, to counter the 'marketization and instrumentalization of standards-based teacher training' (p. 132). Mead describes an information-driven pedagogy that limits trainee and beginning teachers' abilities to critically evaluate such a values-laden policy, which focuses just on facts. Instead, we could be thinking of inquiry-led pedagogy with mentoring and dialogue at its heart.

Goffman (2002), in a seminal work, introduces us to the idea that the self is also dramatic in that we stage ourselves to achieve certain moral ends, which is undoubtedly important to the professional who seeks to contribute to society in his or her own professional context. This is an important learning dimension for the professional who may need to behave in a way that is not always comfortable. For example, the teacher needs to be seen to treat all children equally even if she or he prefers some to others. The general practitioner may find a patient unduly demanding but needs to treat him or her with empathy.

Early model of a good teacher

McArdle and Coutts (2003) developed an early model of the 'good' teacher. This was made explicit and taught to our education student teachers by describing a fun British character known as Mr. Blobby. Mr. Blobby is a rubber suit with a person inside. The rubber suit is voluminous and pink with yellow spots, and the character is unremittingly clumsy and friendly. Mr. Blobby, the rubber suit, cannot move or act without the strong core of a person moving inside.

In our model of the good teacher, the yellow spots on the suit represent experiences, and the strong core, or the person, processes these experiences. For some people, the experiences never reach the strong core. These are the people who do not learn from experience and, in the teaching profession, teach the same class for 30 years without learning, regardless of the needs of the pupils. For other people, the experiences are processed by the strong core to become integrated into the self and the teacher identity.

The strong core is made up of qualities; these qualities were identified from our research in the broad field of adult and teacher education as qualities of strength, confidence, ballast and value maturity. Strength embraces agency and the ability to make things happen. Confidence is a personal quality of positive self-knowledge linked to agency. Ballast is the ability to remain true to professional values and not to be tossed on the waves of vicissitude. Priorities and trends and fashions in teaching come and go, and ballast allows the teacher not to sink under the new demands but to remain true to the values that underpin learning and teaching. Value maturity, linked to ballast, is the knowledge of the personal and professional values that underpin what we do and the integration of these into our behaviour. These strong core qualities enable learning to take place from the experiences that are the yellow spots. On reflection and with the passage of time, we now wish to introduce a new quality to this strong core. The strong core is made up of process qualities – qualities that process experience. We now choose to add 'kindness,' an underpinning virtue that resides in the strong core.

The strong core is useful in assisting with processing and synthesising all the knowledge the teacher needs and has been described in this chapter. The strong core also provides emotional ballast as well as a means of processing experience.

Learning points

1. Teacher knowledge is multi-faceted and includes content knowledge, pedagogical content knowledge, curricular knowledge and general pedagogical knowledge.
2. Content must be selected appropriately, simplified, and connected to teaching strategies, taking into account possible learning difficulties or learning barriers.
3. Language is central to learning.
4. We need to evaluate subject content through the perspective of the child.
5. We need to consider the misconceptions and connections that are likely to be encountered and to allow pupils to experience and understand these at the stage they are at.

Challenge questions

1. What is or has been your favourite topic to teach? Why is this?
2. What is your least favourite subject to teach? Why is this?
3. Thinking about the hierarchy of knowledge, what kind of knowledge do you use mostly in your teaching? Can this be expanded?
4. Thinking of Mr. Blobby, what are some of the yellow spots of experience that were important for you to process in your strong core?

References

ACARA. (2012). Australian curriculum. https://www.australiancurriculum.edu.au/senior-secondary-curriculum/english/english/achievement-standards/

Adoniou, M. (2014). Teacher knowledge: A complex tapestry. *Asia-Pacific Journal of Teacher Education* 43(2), 99–116. https://doi.org/10.1080/1359866X.2014.932330

Ben-Peretz, M. (2011). Teacher knowledge: What is it? How do we uncover it? What are its implications for schooling? *Teaching and Teacher Education* 27, 3–9.

Blömeke, S., Hsieh, F., Kaider, G., Kaiser, G., & Schmidt, W. (Eds.). (2014). *International perspectives on teacher knowledge, beliefs and opportunities to learn: TEDS-M result*. Springer, Dordrecht, Heidelberg, Germany.

Connelly, M., Clandinin, J., & He, M. (1997). Teachers' personal practical knowledge on the professional knowledge landscape. *Teaching and Teacher Education* 13(7), 665–674.

Derewianka, B. (2012). Knowledge about language in the Australian curriculum: English. *Australian Journal of Language and Literacy* 35(1), 127–146.

Goffman, E. (2002, originally published 1959). *The Presentation of Self in Everyday Life*. Garden City, New York.

McArdle, K., & Coutts, N. (2003). A strong core of qualities: A model of the professional educator that moves beyond reflection. *Studies in Continuing Education*, 25(2), 225–238.

McArdle, K., & Hurrell, A. (2016). The man in the rubber suit: A strong core of qualities and the contribution to professional development In T. Norton (Ed.), *Professional development recent advances, future directions* (pp. 197–206). Nova, USA.

Mead, N. (2020). *Values in professional knowledge and in teacher education*. Routledge, Abingdon, Oxfordshire, UK.

Rohaan, E., Taconis, R., & Jochems, W. (2012). Exploring the underlying components of primary school teachers' pedagogical content knowledge for technology education. *International Journal of Technology and Design Education*, 22, 271–280.

Roth, W.-M. (1999). Authentic school science: Intellectual traditions. In R. McCormick & C. Paechter (Eds.), *Learning and knowledge*. Paul Chapman Publishing, Sage, London.

Scheffler, I. (1999). Epistemology and education. In R. McCormick & C. Paechter (Eds.), *Learning and knowledge*. Paul Chapman Publishing, Sage, London.

Shulman, L. S. (1986). Those who understand: Knowledge growth in teaching. *Educational Research*, 15(3), 4e14.

Vygotsky, L. (1978). *Mind in Society: The development of higher psychological processes*. Harvard University Press, Cambridge, UK.

Walshaw, M. (2012). Teacher knowledge as fundamental to effective teaching practice. *The Journal of Mathematics Teacher Education*, 15, 181–185.

Young, M. (1999). The curriculum as socially organised knowledge. *Learning and knowledge*, 56–70. https://books.google.co.uk/books?hl=en&lr=&id=9jwON-NuDtsC&oi=fnd&pg=PA56&dq=Young+M+Curriculum&ots=NIbkD-i5bW&sig=PWXvmYd21tUogOYiGpQ9OeedjNE#v=onepage&q=Young%20M%20Curriculum&f=false

14 Rights

Nothing could be more crucial to democracy than the education of its citizens. Through primary and secondary education, young citizens form, at a crucial age, habits of mind that will be with them all through their lives. They learn to ask questions or not to ask them; to take what they hear at face value or to probe more deeply; to imagine the situation of a person different from themselves or to see a new person as a mere threat to the success of their own projects; to think of themselves as members of a homogeneous group or as members of a nation, and a world, made up of many people and groups, all of whom deserve respect and understanding. So it is not surprising that education has been so emphasized in recent political debates in many developing and developed countries.

Nussbaum, M. (2006, p. 385)

Universal rights

This quotation underscores how important education is to democracy. The *UN Convention on the Rights of the Child (UNCRC)* is an important, legally binding agreement signed by 196 countries (as of 12 July 2022), which outlines the fundamental rights of every child, regardless of their race, religion or abilities. A part of this is quoted as follows:

> **article 28** (right to education)
> Every child has the right to an education. Primary education must be free and different forms of secondary education must be available to every child. Discipline in schools must respect children's dignity and their rights. Richer countries must help poorer countries achieve this.
> **article 29** (goals of education)
> Education must develop every child's personality, talents and abilities to the full. It must encourage the child's respect for human rights, as well as respect for their parents, their own and other cultures, and the environment.
> **article 30** (children from minority or indigenous groups)
> Every child has the right to learn and use the language, customs and religion of their family, whether or not these are shared by the majority of the people in the country where they live.

The Convention has 54 articles that cover all aspects of a child's life and set out the civil, political, economic, social and cultural rights. The convention is universal – these rights apply to every child, and the convention entitles every child to claim them. It also explains how adults and governments must work together to make sure all children can enjoy all their rights.

The Convention came into force in the UK in 1992 (UNICEF, https://www.unicef.org.uk/what-we-do/un-convention-child-rights/ 11/9/2024).

Robeyns (2006) describes how many grand declarations on education are formulated in terms of rights or overall outcome targets without specifying who carries which duty to make sure that these targets are met or that these rights are effectively granted.

Education for democracy

In the light of the whole huge question of how to develop the minds of young children who are going to grow up to be democratic citizens, the emphasis on technology and textbooks that Nussbaum perceives in education seems, she says, to be extremely narrow. She argues that abilities connected with the 'humanities' and the 'arts' are crucial to the formation of citizenship. They must be cultivated if democracies are to survive, through educational policies that focus on pedagogy at least as much as on content.

Three capacities are essential to the cultivation of democratic citizenship in today's world, she suggests. First is a capacity following Socrates, that we may call 'the examined life.' This means a life that accepts no belief as authoritative simply because it has been handed down by tradition or become familiar through habit – a life that questions all beliefs, statements and arguments and accepts only those that survive reason's demand for consistency and for justification. Furthermore, she proposes that this requires developing the capacity to reason logically, to test what one reads or says for consistency of reasoning, correctness of fact and accuracy of judgment; democracy needs citizens who can think for themselves rather than simply deferring to authority, who can reason together about their choices rather than just trading claims and counter-claims.

Second, she suggests, citizens who cultivate their capacity for effective democratic citizenship need an ability to see themselves as not simply citizens of some local region or group but also, and above all, as human beings bound to all other human beings by ties of recognition and concern.

The arts are also crucial sources of both freedom and community, Nussbaum asserts. When people put on a play together, they must learn to go beyond tradition and authority if they are going to express themselves well. And the sort of community created by the arts is non-hierarchical, a valuable model of the responsiveness and interactivity that a good democracy will also foster in its political processes.

Sen (1999) conceptualised wellbeing as flourishing. Equality is conceptualised in terms of the freedoms (or capabilities) that a person has to pursue a valuable life. Education clearly has multiple roles in supporting a life of value, through the opportunities that it provides to develop the sort of valuable functionings that create freedoms for people to do and be whatever they choose. (Spratt, 2017) Whilst the capability approach, which Sen describes, acknowledges that meaningful employment can be one aspect of a valuable life and that money can be a very useful tool for enhancing freedoms, it rejects analyses that see the purpose of human life as entirely economic. Spratt (2017) and we see the purpose as being much wider than this.

The purpose of schooling for Sen is to enhance the freedoms that children have to achieve wellbeing as flourishing. Children develop their capabilities through the 'functionings' that they develop at school. For example, literacy can be seen as a functioning achieved through education that opens the door to a multiplicity of valuable opportunities, and conversely a life without literacy is severely curtailed in its choices. Illiteracy can be seen as an 'unfreedom.' However, in order to develop the freedoms that can be achieved through education, children must have the freedom to access education in the first place.

Amongst the factors that will affect whether and how a child participates in learning experiences is their state of emotional and physical wellbeing (Spratt, 2017). Hence wellbeing can be seen to enhance freedoms in education at two levels. Physical and emotional wellbeing can be seen as functionings that enhance children's capabilities to engage in education, and education in turn develops further functionings that enhance freedoms to flourish through a well-lived life. Of course there is a strong argument that schools and teachers should take account of the physical and emotional wellbeing of their children and play a role in promoting and supporting good health, an acknowledgement of the role that teachers have in responding to children as human beings, recognising where poor physical and emotional wellbeing may impede learning and responding with an appropriate level of care and pedagogical sensitivity.

Rights of the child in practice

Alison presents a conversation she had with parents Ellie and Paul of a child named Lily. Their voice is important in thinking in real terms about the rights of children and parents.

Alison: I was thinking about the chapters in our book, mulling them over in my head: society; leadership; trust; kindness; social justice; humility; courage; well-being; all constructs contingent on our experiences in our own school, our own community, in our own personal and professional background. And then there's the duty of care that we owe to all the children in our classrooms, our playgrounds, our corridors, our classes. This is defined by the United Nations Convention on the Rights of the Child (1989) as 'Promote the rights, including privacy and dignity of children and young people … making sure that they are kept safe from harm, abuse and injury.' This seems so self-evidently true to us as teachers, a corner-stone of all we try to achieve with and for the children we teach. But what if this is not the case and leads to loss of faith in the leadership of the school and of the education system itself?

What follows is a conversation I had with Lily's parents, Ellie and Paul.

So, paint me a picture of Lily, this amazing member of the human race.

E: Before Lily went to school, she was a butterfly. She was incredible. She had such energy and vibrancy. She was playful. She was fearless. She was inquisitive. She was just excited, wasn't she?

P: Yeah. She had a flair then … the way she would be drawn to colour and expressing herself which perhaps sounds a bit strange seeing she was only 4 years old. … I was actually nervous about sending her to school because I felt pretty soon they'd want to put that in a box and she would get extinguished.

Alison: Can I ask why you thought that schooling would change that?

E: I think it's very much a school and society thing.

P: I think the really important thing that a teacher should have in their minds is that when parents send their child to school, they're going to be happy. There has to be a link with the children, getting to know them and understand them, a constant to and fro between them, understanding what the individual wants and listening to them. I do wonder how many teachers are aware of how powerful that can be.

Alison: So when Lily started primary school, her experiences weren't always very happy were they, or is that an overgeneralisation?

E: I can remember it was okay at first, wasn't it? And then there was an experience …. she was told off in the dining hall in front of possibly the whole school and for something she hadn't done. There wasn't any question about what had happened. The teacher just took it on the word of the other two girls saying this is what happened. Didn't ask Lily. Just took it that they were right and basically shamed her. And from that point, that was in P1, she never recovered. She came home that night, and she just would not talk. She just shut down. We literally took weeks to find out what happened, but by then it was too late. It started to build up into something, didn't it? She sort of lost her colour from then, didn't she? It was as if all that she had been able to externalise, all this vibrancy, had just been shut off and sucked in.

P: We described Lily as being this sort of colourful, radiant thing which all of a sudden went to black and white. And that was it. It was horrible really. Lily plays by the rules, she likes to know what the rules are and she has a very straight sense of justice. So the fact that she wasn't even questioned, she didn't actually do anything wrong and was still made to feel like that was … just awful for her. Presumably it meant nothing to anyone else. You know, the teacher was just in a busy hall and trying to shut something down. But in that moment, Lily shut down completely, absolutely devastated, embarrassed, shamed … she was never the same after that.

Alison: Surely that teacher couldn't have been me or any of the teachers I've worked with over many years? Surely not?

The description of Lily as a butterfly by her parents is moving, and also moving to the reader is how this was compromised.

Purpose of education

It is important to think of the purpose of education, and we have asked you to do this explicitly and implicitly in challenge questions throughout this book. We now focus on this more directly as the purpose is the interpretation of children's rights and affects policy and practice in all dimensions of education. There has been a recent tendency to focus on the measurement and comparison of educational outcomes (Biesta, 2009). Writing in 2009, Biesta discusses this, and we consider it still to be the case in 2024/5.

League tables are produced in some countries, with the aim of providing information about the relative performance of schools or school districts and regions. Such league tables have a complicated rationale, says Biesta (2009), combining accountability and choice elements for the government and parents with a social justice argument, which says that everyone should have access to education of the same quality. Unfortunately, this has resulted in a discourse that embraces so-called failing schools and even failing teachers.

Biesta points to an advantage of the measurement culture, namely discussion being based on factual data rather than just opinions. We would argue that data is not always factual or well founded. He does see, however, two problems with this culture.

Biesta (2009) explains that the rise of the measurement culture in education has had a profound impact on educational practice, from the highest levels of educational policy at national and supra-national level down to the practices of local schools and teachers. To some extent this impact has been beneficial as it has allowed for discussions to be based on factual data rather than just assumptions or opinions about what might be the case. The problem is, however, that the abundance of information about educational outcomes has given the impression that decisions about the direction of educational policy and the shape and form of educational practice can be based solely upon factual information. Despite the fact that this is what is happening increasingly in discussions about education in the wake of international comparisons, league tables, accountability, evidence-based education and effective schooling, there are two (obvious) problems with this way of thinking. First, what education is and should be like is based not only on data but on the values of who is making the decision. Second, Biesta suggests, and we agree, that quality indicators can become thought of as the quality of the education itself, meaning quality becomes the end or purpose of education – doing measurement for the sake of doing measurement. The purpose of education is not reliant on the values of just one person. It needs to remain open to discussion in a democratic society.

Biesta (2009) suggests there are three purposes to education:

- Qualification;
- Socialisation;
- Subjectification.

Qualification is about knowledge, skills and understanding, enabling children to do something. Socialisation is about becoming a member of social, political and cultural 'orders.' Subjectification is about what we term critical thinking or independent thinking.

Rights as entitlements

We considered our own view of the purpose of education from the point of view of what the child is entitled to from education and, accordingly, from their teachers. We identified equality in education, fairness, respect, understanding and being listened to and observed. Also, safety, security, consistency, love and care were noted. We also noted that we need to be careful not to be seen as child minding. Relationships with children are crucial. We must be child-centred and role models for children who may, in turn, be role models in their family and the wider community.

John identified his purpose in educating children with additional support needs. He considered the aim to be giving and developing a pace of learning that is right for who the individual child is and where they are in their learning and development, assisting them to develop emotionally socially, academically and in good health. This will lead to providing more opportunities for the children to have more choices in the world and to make positive contributions to society. The children will hence be more independent. One needs to teach the class you have got in front of you rather than just the curriculum. We considered that these purposes are relevant to all children, whatever their needs.

We considered what teachers as colleagues are entitled to in the school and identified support, mutuality, collegiality and an ethos of shared learning. We all recognised situations in staff meetings where people offering new ideas could be glared at because the ideas meant more work. We need a culture of helping and sharing. We consider mentoring to be important, as long as you can choose your own mentor, who hopefully will fill you with excitement and a desire to try new things. Leadership is also important in welcoming new ideas and developing a positive ethos.

Donohoo (2018) contends that in schools, when educators believe in their combined ability to influence student outcomes, there are significantly higher levels of academic achievement (Bandura, 1977). Bandura named this pattern of human behaviour 'collective efficacy,' which he defined as 'a group's shared belief in its conjoint capability to organize and execute the courses of action required to produce given levels of attainment' (Bandura, 1977, p. 477). Donohoo also cites Eells's (2011) meta-analysis of studies related to collective efficacy and achievement in education and demonstrates that the beliefs teachers hold about the ability of the school as a whole are 'strongly and positively associated with student achievement across subject areas and in multiple locations' (p. 110).

So how do school leaders build collective efficacy? Primarily through evidence of impact. When improvement efforts result in improved student outcomes, which are in turn validated through sources of student learning data, the 'collective efficacy' is strengthened. Evidence of collective impact, in turn, reinforces collective behaviours, feelings, thoughts and motivations.

We considered parents' rights too, thinking about these as entitlements. We think that parents have a right to expect that you are getting to know their child and what the child needs to be supported in learning. Above all, they need honesty in the teacher-parent-child relationship. Often parents themselves need support.

One afternoon, a 5-year-old child was having a meltdown at the end of the day outside his classroom. His mother was present, along with members of staff and other children with their families. It was so noticeable that the teaching assistant, who was familiar with the child, stepped in and used her amazing skills of empathy. She also used her ability to set clear boundaries for the child, talking to the child as well as mum. The TA was able to help the parent console the child, using the child's home language, then resolve the situation clearly without it developing further. The parent was subsequently able to walk away with the child hand in hand. This demonstrates innate abilities necessary beyond those often only recognised to teach.

If possible, it is important to be on the same page with parents regarding behaviour, not 'us and them'; we need to be collaborating to improve behaviour. So many parents have had a bad experience of school, and it may be a big achievement for them to go through the door of the school to see a teacher. They may think they need a special language to talk to teachers as they are not confident about how to ask questions and perhaps think they cannot do maths themselves. Schools still have a touch of authority and can terrify some people.

The issue of homework is very complex for parents and teachers alike. Children may be tired after school. Muslim children may go to the mosque for an hour and a half or thereabouts after school and so have little time for homework. Where both parents are working, the child may be out of their house from 7.30 am till 6.00 pm. Homework can be a choice for children. If it is compulsory, you have to decide what to do if they do not complete it or an older sibling does it, for example. Some parents like homework as they can stay in touch with the child's learning. Alison chose to make homework a choice for children and invited parents to sit in class if they wished to know what their child was learning. Increasingly schools are being encouraged to open their doors to parents and the community. It is important to think about what homework is for and what is its impact. Perhaps it is rather a sexist hangover from a past when generally one parent was at home.

We thought about the individual teacher and what she or he is entitled to. A long search of academic literature found nothing about rights for teachers. There was a lot about responsibilities. Rubrics of teaching practice generally started with the phase, 'the teacher must. ... ' We thought about what exists and found rights in employment law, trade unions and the right to collective action. We were aware of investigations into violence in schools and consider teachers to have a right not to be abused.

We also think teachers should have a right to time for planning, thinking and reflecting. In Penny's school they teach for nine days over two weeks. This is called PPA time (planning, preparation and assessment time). All English schools provide teachers this time, but up till now most schools offer an afternoon or a morning a week. However, having a whole day every two weeks is a lot more time and energy efficient. This refreshes the teacher, Penny says, with all the benefits that implies.

Opportunities for support and supervision need to be more than annual, in our opinion. Teachers should be entitled to equality and a greater quantity and quality of continuing professional development. We wish teachers to have wellbeing and to feel happy within themselves when teaching. This implies reducing the stress of too much teaching, which can contribute to silo thinking and practice. Linked to this is the need for new initiatives to be reasonable in their demands on teachers. It takes courage not to do initiatives if there are too many, and it is risky because inspectors of education maybe looking for these in their scrutiny.

We are aware of new initiatives that can be ill thought through, such as a recent initiative that resulted in year 9 (age 14) children's maths being taught to year 6 (age 11-12). This pressure can result in burnout and a lack of work-life balance. We accordingly consider that teachers need a right to a stronger voice in decision making about education initiatives and a right to be heard at national levels in particular.

Learning points

1. One of the purposes of schooling is to enhance the freedoms that children have to achieve wellbeing as flourishing.
2. We have a responsibility to respond to children as human beings, recognising where poor physical and emotional wellbeing may impede learning and responding with an appropriate level of care and pedagogical sensitivity.
3. We need to teach the class we have in front of us rather than simply covering, or delivering, the curriculum.
4. Teachers as colleagues are entitled to support, mutuality, collegiality and an ethos of shared learning.
5. Parents have a right to expect that we are getting to know their child and what the child needs to be supported in learning.
6. Teachers need a right to a stronger voice in decision making about education initiatives and also a right to be heard at national levels in particular.

Challenge questions

1. How do you let the children know that you care about them as individuals?
2. Identify a time when you worked collegially. What benefits were there to you and to the school?
3. How do you identify the learning needs of the children in your class?
4. How do you identify their needs in relation to well-being and happiness?
5. How might teachers voice their opinions of education initiatives at a school level?

References

Bandura, A. (1977). Self-efficacy: Toward a unifying theory of behavioural change. *Psychological Review* 84(2), 191-215.

Biesta, G. (2009). Good education in an age of measurement: On the need to reconnect with the question of purpose in education. *Educational Assessment, Evaluation and Accountability* 21, 33-46. https://doi.org/10.1007/s11092-008-9064-9

Donohoo, J., Hattie, J., & Eells, R. (2018). The power of collective efficacy. *Educational Leadership* 75(6), 40-44.

Eells, R. (2011). *Meta-analysis of the relationship between collective efficacy and student achievement.* Unpublished doctoral dissertation. Loyola University of Chicago.

Nussbaum, M. C. (2006). Education and democratic citizenship: Capabilities and quality education. *Journal of Human Development* 7(3), 385-395. https://doi.org/10.1080/14649880600815974

Robeyns, I. (2006). The search for new policy principles and the possibilities and problems of a capabilities approach. *Economy and Society* 34, 76-104.

Sen, A. (1999). *Development as freedom.* Oxford University Press, Oxford.

Spratt, J. (2017). Wellbeing, equity and education. In *A critical analysis of policy discourses of wellbeing in schools.* Cham, Switzerland: Springer.

15 Social justice
Gaps in society

Introduction

Thinking about social justice leads inevitably to thinking about social problems, in particular poverty. Rawls (2004, p. 51) explains how a social idea of fairness or justice is connected with 'a conception of society, a vision of the way in which the aims and purposes of social cooperation are to be understood.' Social justice is about the way some people experience the world in comparison to others and is closely linked to ideas about human rights. Alison describes the rights of the child and the link to the future of libraries in the UK, many of which are currently being closed to save money.

The United Nations Convention on the Rights of the Child (1989) stresses the right of every child to the development of his or her full potential, the right to free and open access to information, materials and programmes, under equal conditions for all, irrespective of age, race, sex, religious, national and cultural background, language, social status or personal skills and abilities.

Where better to ensure these rights than in libraries?

People of Alison's generation took them for granted as children, teenagers and adults as places where we could meet up with friends of both sexes at the weekend, safely, watched over by the library staff; pre-digital age, we greedily opened encyclopaedias, sharing parts of our culture with chums: Who lived where in the world, who ate what and why, who dressed how and why, who prayed where; and then the atlases, with huge parts of the world covered in pink – why was that?

Sometimes we went to the library with our parents and we learned to sit quietly with our noses in our favourite author, mindful not to disturb others. Sometimes we saw older people reading the newspapers, sitting for hours in the warmth, without us wondering why; mums (mainly) reading stories to their wee ones; immigrant families meeting together, with what we then thought of as 'strange' languages permeating the air – our first contact with a social conscience, perhaps.

So, what are children being denied now? Why are local authorities closing down libraries, often in the most deprived socioeconomic areas of our towns? Who is advocating for the rights of the children, if it is not the very politicians and councillors who claim that education is a national priority? What do they consider the purposes of education to be if not that all pupils should learn? They should learn not just the curriculum but the development of values and beliefs that help society to include everyone fairly, equitably and respectfully.

Of course, there are digital resources – search engines, podcasts, webchats, school homework being posted and marked online and this is, after all, only part of the evolutionary cycle. But I would posit that school children and others are missing out on so much more! I'm all for evolution, but I'm a great fan of revolution as well!

Teachers have a voice, and we must use that voice to protect and promote the United Nations Convention on The Rights of the Child. We cannot, and I would suggest we should not, allow the tenets of the convention to slip into rhetoric and inaction.

You only need to look at any classroom to see that some children are from better-off families than others. Some may be dressed better and be cleaner; some may have more toys or an expensive phone. Many schools do not encourage children to bring in toys to avoid jealousy, envy or feeling 'poor.' Social justice in the school is about treating all children the same but also working actively to minimise injustice. Anderson (2004) says the aim of being equal is not to eliminate the impact of 'brute luck' (being born into the wrong family) but to 'end oppression, which is socially imposed' (p. 155). Its proper purpose, she says, is to create a community in which people stand in relations of equality to others. She describes equality as a relationship among people, as well as a pattern of the distribution of goods or resources. She also considers respect for citizens in a policy context. A society that permits its members to sink to depths hardly treats them with respect. Free breakfasts and breakfast clubs are common in the UK to make sure all children eat at least one good meal a day, and some schools have free swimming lessons to protect the safety of all children. The need for social justice covers all dimensions of education. Thinking about assessment, in England schools are required to meet Ofqual's regulatory framework, which is about *inter alia* social justice and states, for example, 'assessment should minimise bias, differentiating only on the basis of each pupil's level of attainment. A pupil should not be disadvantaged by factors that do not relate to what is being tested' (EYF, 2023, p. 46).

Neo-liberalism

Neo-liberalism is an ideology that we consider has had in the past, and continues to have, an impact on wealthy Western nations and through these countries' actions an impact on poorer nations elsewhere. It is an idea that some argue underpins the curriculum we teach, as well as the systems and structures of education. Neo-liberalism is an ideology characterised by a belief in sustained economic growth as the means to achieve human progress, confidence in free markets as the most efficient means of allocation of resources, emphasis on minimal state intervention in economic and social affairs, and commitment to the freedom of trade and capital.

Neo-liberalism has its origins in the 18th century with the publication of Adam Smith's *Wealth of Nations*. It is difficult to find in the literature contributions that justify neo-liberalism. Yet the underpinning ideology is apparent in policy, political speeches and educational practice. We make no apology for our criticism of neo-liberalism; it is not just an economic idea but also, as Imogen Tyler (2021) puts it, a social idea. It embraces a form of 'governance through which public consent is procured for policies and practices that effect inequalities and fundamentally corrode democracy' (p. 5).

The history of neo-liberalism is well described by Ledwith and Springett (2022). Essentially, in 1947 in Switzerland, a group of men came up with the ideology that Ledwith and Springett suggest 'would replace cooperation and compassion with competition and exploitation' (2022, p. 44). It is evident in right-wing populist politics in the United States and the UK. Ledwith and Springett (2022) describe how the right wing of politics postures to the poor by claiming to believe in the people, nationhood and culture, whilst at the same time 'reaping the harvest of the injustices of poverty, inequality and discrimination ...' that goes with the ideology (p. 49).

> The current global dominant narrative, neoliberal capitalism, based on values of competition, status and individualism gives rise to excessive greed and consumption which inevitably creates extreme social inequalities and causes ecological destruction.
> (Ledwith & Springett, 2022, p. 198)

This quotation should make us, as educators, think about whether and how we promote in the classroom competition, status and individualism rather than community. It is impossible to think of social justice without thinking of injustice. Dorling's (2015) five tenets of injustice, discussed in Chapter 1 of this book and derived from his book *Injustice: Why Social Inequality Still Exists*, are illustrated with statistics for the UK and USA, in particular. The five tenets are reasons or justifications for a common-sense understanding of inequality, often propounded within the neo-liberal ideology.

- Elitism is efficient;
- Exclusion is necessary;
- Prejudice is natural;
- Greed is good;
- Despair (for some) is inevitable.

These five tenets can be viewed as assumptions about the way the world is and as being immutable.

Tyler (2021) describes how neo-liberalism has contributed to dimensions of social injustice, citing how governments have come to govern *for* the markets but *against* the people. She describes how Britain has witnessed an erosion of workers' rights, civil liberties and human rights, which are seen to block market competition. She cites Harvey (2005), who argues neo-liberalism is a class project, 'an ideology, which aims to restore and consolidate class power, under the veil of the rhetoric of individualism, choice, freedom, mobility and national security' (p. 7).

> Those of us who can afford it fortify ourselves against all visible and invisible, present or anticipated, known or still unfamiliar, diffuse but ubiquitous dangers, through locking ourselves in behind walls, stuffing the approaches to our living quarters with TV cameras, hiring armed guards, driving armoured vehicles (such as the notorious SUVs) wearing armoured clothing (like 'big-soled shoes') or taking martial arts classes.
> (Bauman, 2005, p. 69)

Tyler (2021) argues that a major characteristic of neo-liberal democracies is that they function through the generation of fear and anxiety rather than fidelity to national identity.

Once again we refer to the United Nations Convention on the Rights of the Child (1989) stresses the right of every child to the development of his or her full potential, the right to free and open access to information, materials and programmes, under equal conditions for all, irrespective of age, race, sex, religious, national and cultural background, language, social status or personal skills and abilities.

Hegemony, power and social justice

Hegemony may be thought of as the dominance of one group over another through the legitimisation of dominating norms and ideas, often through public consent. Social control is maintained through persuasion, not overt force.

Hegemony for Gramsci was about the cultural and moral dimensions of the exercise of political power (1971). Hegemony is constructed though mechanisms of political negotiation and intellectual persuasion (Hoare & Sperber, 2016). The media play an important role in the idea of hegemony, often playing to the fears and anxieties, and indeed prejudices, of people, as doing so sells papers and programmes. This mirroring of fear serves to reinforce these fears and often contributes, we propose, to prejudice.

Examples of hegemony in practice can be seen in Dorling's five tenets of injustice. 'Greed is good' and 'despair is inevitable' are messages that are presented as truths and can be accepted as truths rather than thinking about the social, cultural, moral and economic assumptions that underpin these supposed truths.

Power and social justice

Power, or lack of it, is an idea closely linked to the concept of social justice. Michel Foucault, a French philosopher, is very influential in thinking about power. He saw power as not being something some people have and others do not. Rather he saw it as being in every transaction in life between people, so power is beyond systems and structures. He was preoccupied with how people can become conscious and free themselves from power structures and false consciousness (Ledwith & Springett, 2022). Power relations, according to the French philosopher Michel Foucault, are embedded in discourse, or the narratives that are created around ideas, such as education, religion, criminal justice and the behaviours that discourse engenders in people.

> Power is not something that is acquired, seized or shared, something that one holds onto or allows to slip away; power is exercised from innumerable points, in the interplay of nonegalitarian and mobile relations.
>
> (Foucault, 1998/1976, p. 94)

Foucault believed that we are always inside power; there is no escaping it.

Like Freire, Foucault believed people could overcome false consciousness, as Foucault described it. We choose to discuss this here as critical reflection. Critical means the ability to be transformative, to lead to fundamental changes in perspective (Fook, 2010). Critical also implies a focus on hegemonic perspectives. Critical reflection enables an understanding of the ways in which society's systems and structures, individuals and groups may be socially restrictive. This it is thought to lead to empowering ideas and behaviours. Critical reflection involves, for example, how people engage with the world, how they construct a sense of identity and how they construct personal meanings (Fook, 2010).

What we can do about social justice

Thinking about social justice is important but can make the educator feel the problems are too big or too political for them to tackle. We suggest moving beyond equating social justice with simple equality in practice.

We propose the need for:

- Counter-hegemony and critical education;
- Sharpening up of our language and speaking truth to power;
- Amplifying and interpreting voice and stories.

Counter-hegemony sees changed thinking and changed action as part of the same process. This is important because hegemony is experienced as 'an internalised reality, which is both understood and felt, it is not just an abstract structure' (Beck & Purcell, 2020, p. 59). Hegemony makes people see things that may oppress them as normal, so counter-hegemony or change can challenge both feeling and thinking of children where we see injustice. Hegemony asserts control over knowledge and culture, affirming the ideas of the dominant culture and inevitably marginalising and silencing others (Ledwith & Springett, 2022). Counter-hegemony is change that reshapes the balance of social power away from ruling elites into the hands of people who are marginalised (Beck & Purcell, 2020). Changes in class consciousness are necessary for transformative change, and this change is a psychological process that Gramsci sees as cathartic (Hoare & Sperber, 2016). It comes about through a number of actions. Stimulating critical thinking in self, colleagues and children and reflection assist people to see that the normal balance of power may indeed be oppressive and that things could be different.

Collective action assists with overcoming the sense of loneliness or not belonging that can go with being oppressed; it also lays the foundations for action to achieve change. Beck and Purcell (2020) argue that we can assist with developing links locally, nationally and internationally as we live in a globalised society. Most recently, political literacy or helping others learn how to be heard is one way of assisting with both critical thinking and collective action.

Sharpening up our language means telling it as we see it, and perhaps seeing things more plainly. Here Chapter 6, Courage, is helpful. 'Black lives matter,' as a phrase, is so much stronger than speaking about racial equality. It is so easy for decision makers to hide behind the bland language of inclusion and equality without doing very much differently. We suggest it is the role of the teacher to speak truth to power and to discuss discrimination and injustice where it exists. Rather than speaking of food insecurity in school, for example, we can speak of hunger and prevent decision makers from hiding from the truth. This demands courage as it will not be popular, but it is integral to the values that underpin the profession.

Amplifying and interpreting voice and story are crucial as a response to social justice. The voice of our pupils can be amplified, placed in a context and interpreted by us for decision makers. A story of a child in a family having to choose whether to eat or heat the house can be illuminating for decision makers. We can also act to eliminate the problems of hunger in practical ways in the school. It is important to note that the impact of neo-liberalism and hegemony affects us as well as our pupils.

Learning points

1. Social justice is closely linked to ideas about injustice and the gaps in society between the haves and have nots.
2. Neo-liberalism is an ideology that has an impact on the gaps in society, namely widening them.
3. Methods of countering meo-liberalism include:

   - Counter-hegemony and critical education;
   - Sharpening up of our language and speaking truth to power;
   - Amplifying and interpreting voice and stories.

Challenge questions

1. Have you noticed a difference in your classroom between the 'haves' and 'have nots'? Do you think this matters, and it is part of your role as a teacher to manage this?
2. Is there a difference in behaviour or abilities? Why is this?
3. How do you behave with the different groups? Why is this?
4. What is done in your school to make things more equal?
5. Can you think of anything else that you could do or could be done to tackle social justice?

References

Anderson, E. S. (2004). Against luck egalitarianism: What is the point of equality? In M. Clayton & A. Williams (Eds.), *Social justice*. Blackwell Publishing, Malden, MA.
Bauman, Z. (2005). *Liquid life*. Polity Press, Cambridge, UK.
Beck, D., & Purcell, R. (2020). *Community development for social change*. Routledge, New York, NY.
Dorling, D. (2015). *Injustice: Why social inequality still persists*. Policy Press, Bristol, UK.
Early Years Foundation Stage (EYFS). (2023, December; effective 4 January 2024 2023). *Statutory framework for group and school-based providers. Setting the standards for learning, development and care for children from birth to five*. Westminster Government, London.
Fook, J. (2010). Beyond reflective practice: Reworking the 'critical' in critical reflection. In H. Bradbury, N. Frost, S. Kilminster, & M. Zukas (Eds.), *Beyond reflective practice: Mew approaches to professional lifelong learning*. Routledge, Abingdon, Oxon, UK.
Foucault, M. (1998, originally published 1976). *The will to knowledge: The history of sexuality: 1*. Trans. R. Hurley. Penguin Books, London.
Gramsci, A. (1971). *Selections from prison notebooks*. International Publishers, New York, USA
Harvey, D. (2005). *A brief history of neoliberalism*. Oxford University Press, Oxford, UK.

Hoare, G., & Sperber, N. (2016). *An Introduction to Antonio Gramsci: His life, thought and legacy*. Bloomsbury, London.
Ledwith, M., & Springett, J. (2022). *Participatory practice: Community-based action for transformative change*. Policy Press, Bristol.
Rawls, J. (2004, originally published 1999). On justice as fairness. In M. Clayton & A. Williams (Eds.), *Social justice*. Blackwell Publishing, Malden, MA.
Tyler, I. (2021). *Revolting subjects: Social abjection and resistance in neoliberal Britain*. Zed Books Bloomsbury, London.
UNICEF. (1989). Convention on the rights of the child. https://scholar.google.com/scholar?hl=en&as_sdt=0%2C5&q=Un+Convetion+on+he+Rights+of+theevHild&btnG=#d=gs_cit&t=1756026894420&u=%2Fscholar%3Fq%3Dinfo%3Aumo8TcyjuEgJ%3Ascholar.google.com%2F%26output%3Dcite%26scirp%3D3%26hl%3Den

PART FOUR

In this final section, we consider how you can move forward with the ideas that we have presented. You cannot change all at once, so we suggest setting priorities. We also present the conclusions we have reached whilst writing this book, which we hope you are enjoying reading.

16 Moving forward

We teach who we are 'in times of darkness as well as light.'

(Palmer, 2017, p. xix)

Introduction

It is one thing to read a book, yet another to put it into practice. In this chapter we focus on how to make the ideas in the book work for you.

The first thing to think about is that becoming a very good teacher does not happen all at once. We need to practise and to practise improving every day. Every good teacher is good in different ways, so we hope you will find a way to express yourself and your individuality through your teaching, and to be kind to yourself as you learn and learning takes place throughout your career. Times change, we change, and children change over time, and this too requires learning and adaptation so our work in progress of becoming a good teacher never ends. We hope you will be joyful and joyous as a teacher about what you are good at. We hope the changes you face are not frightening or anxiety provoking. Among the approaches to becoming a very good teacher is not to think only of what you want to do with the children as activities; think instead about the children first. What do they need and want from learning? How is the curriculum best interpreted for your class?

Thinking about self in the school, we think it is good to be collaborative, to be open and grounded and not the 'curmudgeon in the corner' at staff meetings who always says it will not work. Time is needed to talk about teaching with others and to model good practice. New initiatives arise quite often and can disappear after a short time. If they are worthwhile, they need time to be embedded. Similarly, teachers need time to unpick and repack in response to new ideas. As highlighted in the epigraph by Palmer, we need to be adaptable and flexible to our surroundings and situation, going with the flow of new ideas and hopefully having a good team to support each other.

The context in which you teach is very important. Opportunities for growth and reflection need to come from the school. Teachers need to establish for themselves the values of the educational system and the school itself. What are the stated values, and what are the lived values and are these the same? Also, we consider discussing teaching to be very important. Teaching and teacher education are considered by some people to have become 'de-philosophised,' so that teachers do not have the resources or inclination to discuss pedagogy together.

DOI: 10.4324/9781032678283-20

Thinking again of new initiatives, the key question to ask is what is the pedagogical justification for this? Sometimes, we suggest, it seems this question has not been asked.

Who we are – Pierre Bourdieu: Habitus and field

Maton (2012) describes a concept called 'habitus,' which is a term used by French philosopher Pierre Bourdieu, who has written deeply about practice. Habitus focuses on our ways of acting, thinking, feeling and being but, most importantly, focuses on our history, how we carry it in ourselves and how we bring this history into our present or current behaviour. We are in an ongoing and active process of making history, but not under conditions entirely of our own making. Habitus is the baggage we have acquired; it has become incorporated in ourselves in the form of permanent dispositions, or ways of thinking, feeling and acting. Our habitus will affect who we are and how we choose to practice.

Maton (2012) goes on to say that sometimes the context in which we work changes more quickly than or in different directions to the habitus of its members. The practice we have can then seem anachronistic, stubbornly resistant or ill-informed.

'Field' is another term used by Bourdieu to describe the social space in which interactions, transactions and events occur (Thomson, 2012). Analysing a social space like a school or classroom involves locating it in a specific historical, local, national and international context and also looking at the ways in which previous knowledge about the school has been generated, by whom, and whose interests were served by the knowledge generation practices.

Like games, fields have unspoken rules and roles that people play, such as set positions on a football field. Fields, says Thomson (2012), have their own rules, histories, star players, legends and lore (p. 67) and, we would add, so do schools. Thinking about your school as a 'field' will help you to understand your role. Fuller (2012) says, obviously, the function of schools is to teach and socialize students, but Bourdieu points out that schools teach students in particular ways and also socialize them in particular ways.

Deer (2021) explains that 'reflexivity' is important in thinking about social situations. Reflexivity we define as challenging taken-for-granted assumptions. We need to think about what we do, who we do it with, when we do it, where we do it and how. Bourdieu thinks language is very important in thinking about habitus and field. We can ask questions about the use of language in our schools. What exactly is meant and practised in the name of diversity, for example? Or what is meant and intended by school exclusion, and what does it mean for staff, the pupil and parents or carers?

Moving forward, we hope you will be considering what there is in your history or habitus that affects what you believe and do in education. We also hope you will be thinking about the field environment of a school you know and the language that is used in that environment, whilst you are challenging taken-for-granted assumptions.

Identity and self-awareness, once again

In this book so far, we have suggested lots of things you should do or be. Self-awareness is crucial to learning and being a good teacher. The first thing we think you should be aware of is that you *can* teach and learning how to teach is never ending. We learn all the time to develop an increasingly rich repertoire of skills, qualities and knowledge. We think it is important to know that teaching is not simply about imparting knowledge to the children; rather it is about knowing the different learning needs of all the children in your class. Our experience suggests that some teachers are daunted by the prospect of being child-centred with a class of 32 children. Practically, the relationship you have built with one child can signal how the whole class is responding. It is about finding balance a lot of the time between meeting individual needs and working with the class as a whole.

Observation, noticing and listening are crucial to being a good teacher, and they are linked to knowing self. If the children are not engaged in, for example, doing maths and teaching about protractors, slow down! Maths, in particular, relies on building concepts on top of each other. If the children are fidgeting or glazed, approach the subject from 360 degrees, finding different ways to communicate if one is not working. When you are a beginning teacher, you can have back-up plans for your lesson. The more experienced teacher will be 'reflecting in action.' This is discussed later in this chapter.

One of the challenges we have as teachers is the ability to be self-aware; some may not be as critically self-aware as others. This example was relayed to Penny by the class teacher, who was working with the student teacher at the time. Many years ago, a trainee teacher was so focussed on her subject (preparation was excellent, with slides, work sheets and artefacts), they forgot about the essentials of teaching - pupil engagement, effective classroom management and effective communication with the pupils.

The lesson started well, when the class teacher was in the room. However, as soon as the teacher left the room, teaching about the Romans became harder, although the trainee teacher was not aware of this. Unfortunately, spending too long on the introduction, with little self-awareness of her pupils' lack of interest, made the 8- and 9-year-olds more restless and fidgety. A particular child, who was an enthusiastic learner, but only on his terms, decided this lesson wasn't for him. So, he decided to tap his pen to alert the trainee's attention, with no response; his next step was to wander around the room, annoying other pupils, which the trainee seemed oblivious to; when asked about this later, she felt it was more important to deliver the Roman project.

The pupil continued to disturb others but then started opening a window, thinking it would be a good idea to demonstrate his climbing skills. It was only then that another child ran out of the room to find the class teacher to explain what was happening. They both returned to prevent the nimble pupil from clambering out of the classroom from a first-floor window.

The trainee teacher had only noticed a problem when the class teacher ran over to the child at the window. Meanwhile, she had continued to deliver her message of the Romans in Britain. This demonstrates the importance of self-awareness before we teach pupils and of how essential it is to be aware of the children's varied needs. If we are self-aware as teachers, we are more likely to deliver successful lessons, with active engagement and enjoyment.

The repertoire of the experienced teacher keeps expanding. You may remember that we all learn through play, and if things are not working, play is useful. Teaching grammar for example can be done in pairs or triads, with different words in envelopes and the children making up sentences with the words and reading them out to see if they make sense.

Smith (2010) suggests the nature of personhood, what we describe as self, is complicated but also ultimately mysterious, and thinking about self raises a host of practical moral and ethical questions. Smith discusses causal capacities or the powers that facilitate the human being to bring about change in 'material or mental phenomena, to produce or influence objects and events in the world' (p. 42). Smith comes up with 30 capacities we have that promote this.

The first capacity mentioned is consciousness that we share with many other living creatures. The second capacity is 'unconscious being.' Not all the desires, feelings, beliefs, dispositions and goals are immediately accessible to the conscious mind, and we suggest they require some work to bring them to conscious attention. This capacity is linked to 'practical consciousness,' which means the ability to go on in life without thinking exactly how and why one is doing so. This is also known as 'tacit knowledge.' (Polanyi, 1962) explains that we can know more than we can tell.

Emotions are cited as one of the 30 capacities. We do not merely feel pain or anger like other animals; we are able to 'enjoy and suffer extremely profound, complicated, and overwhelming affective events of feeling, emotion, mood, sentiment and passion' (Smith, p. 46). They have profound consequences for perception, motivation and behaviour. Creativity, innovation and imagination are cited as a capacity by Smith (p. 46). People can 'mentally innovate' (Smith, p. 47) to visualise, dream, invent, connect, conceive and envision ideas, possibilities and images that do not yet exist in reality.'

Particularly Important to teaching, in our opinion, is what Smith describes as 'self-transcendence' (Smith, p. 49). This is the profound ability to pass beyond our own interests to be attentive and present to other people. Smith describes this as extraordinary and profound, because we are putting aside the great subjective depths of self-concern to devote ourselves to things above and beyond ourselves.

Finally, we shall look at Smith's description of identity formation and self-reflexivity as capacities that we consider to be central to moving forwards as a self-aware teacher. We have what Smith describes as reflexive perceptions of ourselves as more or less unique creatures, representing particular character traits, personality, psychological structure and social location 'that are relatively durable, defining of self, and behaviour-guiding' (Smith, p. 50). Self-reflexivity is when people make themselves the subject of their own reflection and evaluation. Self-reflexivity is linked to forming virtues. As Smith puts it, 'humans have the capacity to purposefully integrate a variety of their beliefs, desires, and actions into stable dispositions and habits to think and act in certain ways and under certain circumstances in order to foster lives of greater happiness and moral goodness' (Smith, p. 52).

We consider that courage and criticality are important to self-awareness. Courage is discussed in Chapter 6 and criticality in Chapter 2. Courage is needed because we can never be sure how our self-concept will be challenged by self-awareness (McArdle & Hurrell, 2016). Holstein and Gubrium (2000) suggest, cradle to grave, we refer to ourselves to make sense of our conduct and experience and to guide related actions. The self is not only something we are but is an object we actively construct and live by. We direct behaviour to others, and their responses help define who we are. So, we ask, how does one go about processing our experiences that influence our behaviour? We suggest that we need a strong core to process experiences. This strong core is made up of qualities of strength, confidence, ballast and value-maturity (McArdle & Hurrell, 2016). Ballast is the ability to remain true to values and not to be tossed on the waves of vicissitude. Priorities, trends and fashions come and go in teaching, and ballast allows the teacher to remain true to values that underpin learning and teaching.

Self-assessment is part of self-awareness. Mezirow & Associates (2000) describe the uses of self-assessment. 'It can be used to:

- self-monitor and check progress;
- promote good learning practices (learn how to learn);
- self-diagnose and self-remediate;
- practice (sic) alternatives to other forms of assessment;
- improve professional or academic practice;
- consolidate learning over a range of contexts;
- review achievements as a prelude to recognising prior learning;
- achieve self-knowledge and self-understanding.'

(pp. 178–9)

Mezirow & Associates (2000) describe learning as transformation, with learning occurring in one of four ways: by elaborating existing frames of reference, by learning new frames of reference, by transforming points of view or by transforming habits of mind. Transformation often follows some variation, he says, of the following phases of meaning becoming clear:

1. A disorientating dilemma;
2. Self-examination with feelings of fear, anger, guilt or shame;
3. A critical assessment of assumptions;
4. Recognition that one's discontent and the process of transformation are shared;
5. Exploration of options for new roles, relationships and actions;
6. Planning a course of action;
7. Acquiring knowledge and skills for implementing one's plans;
8. Provisional trying of new roles;
9. Building competence and self-confidence in new role and relationships;
10. A reintegration into one's life on the basis of conditions dictated by one's new perspective.

(Mezirow & Associates, 2000, p. 22)

Self-awareness in the teaching context comes through many different ways of learning about oneself. Here, we focus on critical thinking and learning through reflection, the latter having been a frequently occurring theme in this book.

Critical reflection and reflexivity again

Reflection is:

> A complex activity aimed at investigating one's own action in a certain situation and involving a review of the experience, an analysis of causes and effects, and the drawing of conclusions concerning future action, and which results in a changed conceptual perspective.

(Hoyrup & Elkjaer, 2016, p. 29)

Reflection can be individual, critical in which the individual reflects on the social and political premises or assumptions. It can be collective as well as organisational, where the focus is on systems and structures (Hoyrup & Elkjaer, 2016).

Reflection is often stimulated by disturbance and uncertainty. Hoyrup and Elkjaer (2016) describe the process:

1. **Definition of the problem**: This means developing a possible hypothesis for explanation of the troubling situation.
2. **Formation of guiding concepts or ideas**: This means identifying the ideas that underpin the problem.
3. **Elaboration of ideas**: For Dewey (1986) the heart of reflection lies in inquiry into former experiences and connections and accordingly, continuities of experiences are established.
4. **Testing**: Here the guiding ideas or concepts are tested in action by working out a solution in practice.

(Hoyrup & Elkjaer, 2016, pp. 30-31)

Critical reflection is a way of standing back and learning about things from a new perspective rather than just dwelling on or thinking about things. It is also a way of articulating explicitly the value of knowledge generated from your own experience (Fook & Gardner, 2007). Critical reflection seeks to unsettle and challenge taken-for-granted assumptions. It is about developing changes in practice from an awareness of our professional context.

The broad purpose of critical reflection, according to Fook and Gardner (2007), is:

- To develop professional practice theory;
- To research professional practice;
- To evaluate professional practice;
- To change professional practice from a critical perspective;
- To learn directly from professional practice experience.

Critical reflection with others helps to challenge taken-for-granted assumptions and shared identification of changes to practice.

Frost (2010) suggests reflection is seen as something that happens in the head, and thus the role of the wider social environment is underplayed. Boud (2010) emphasizes the need to locate reflection in the context of practice, including in the courses that prepare the professional for this practice. Thinking about practice, David Boud (2010) suggests that practice is necessarily contextualised. It does not exist apart from a particular setting; it is not meaningful to discuss practice disaggregated from practice settings, as it loses many dimensions. Also, practice is embodied in practitioners, the whole person. This attitude suggests that reflection needs to take place in the practitioner environment, particularly as pupils are increasingly being regarded as co-practitioners, in that they co-produce knowledge about themselves.

Fook (2010) summarises why reflection should be critical: First, its focus on unearthing deep assumptions and, second, because of its focus on power dynamics.

> Critical reflection ... is reflection which enables an understanding of the way socially dominant assumptions may be socially restrictive and this enables new, more empowering ideas and practices. Critical reflection thus enables social change.
>
> (Fook, 2010, p. 40)

There is of course a link to teacher agency in enabling social change (see Chapter 10). Collier (2010) discusses the role of imagination and creativity in reflection. She sees a danger in reflection becoming too instrumental and suggests the arts and imaginative processes that can be introduced to reflection. The arts perspective can offer a framework that gives form and significance to imaginative thought.

Professional artistry

In our experience good teachers must and do reflect well *in* action as well as *on* action. Reflection in action is being surprised, thinking on your feet and experimenting with new action.

Schön (1987) uses the term 'professional artistry' to refer to:

> the kinds of competence practitioners sometimes display in unique, uncertain and conflicted situations. Note, however, that their artistry is a high-powered esoteric variant of the more familiar sort of competence all of us exhibit every day in countless acts of recognition, judgement and skilful performance. What is striking about both kinds of competence is that they do not depend on our being able to describe what we know how to do or even to entertain in conscious thought the knowledge our actions reveal.
>
> (Schön, 1987, p. 22)

When we have learnt how to do something, explains Schön, we can execute 'smooth sequences of activity, recognition, decision and adjustment' (p. 26) without having to think about it explicitly.

Reflexivity

Reflexivity is related to reflection and involves recognising the influence of self in a context. It is a 'turning-back' (like a reflex angle in geometry) on oneself. So, to be reflexive, we need to be aware of the many and varied ways in which we might create or at least Influence the knowledge that we use (Fook & Gardner, 2007).

Reflexivity is the ability to recognise that *all* aspects of ourselves and our contexts influence the way we create knowledge. Reflexivity is useful in reflection for:

- Awareness of ourselves as creators of knowledge directly from practice;
- A focus on assumptions about knowledge and its creation.

(Fook & Gardner, 2007, p. 31)

Some of the best ways of raising self-awareness involve working with others. We can learn from colleagues, from the headteacher and from the children.

Role modelling

Role modelling is an important way that we learn to be who we are professionally, and it also is important for senior staff in the organisation to provide leadership in appropriate and desirable behaviour (McArdle & Hurrell, 2016). The appropriate use of role models gives permission for the admission of difficult experiences. Role modelling allows colleagues to act as equals and to learn from each other rather than only from above. For role modelling to work a culture or ethos of working positively to support and celebrate good practice is vital. The following quotation implies that role models know their own 'bigger picture,' their values in action, their belief system and their personal and professional identities. You will remember this balance of qualities was discussed in Chapter 2.

> A model is someone who demonstrates new ways of living ... someone who remains loving and humble ... someone who does not judge or condemn. Through their lives, these people show us the bigger picture.
>
> (Vanier, 1998, p. 131)

McArdle and Hurrell (2016) describe further key characteristics of effective models (pp. 201-2):

> Personal qualities (savoir-être) include attributes that promote learning in other professionals, such as compassion, honesty, kindness and integrity. Effective interpersonal relationships, enthusiasm for practice; for the profession of educating others; and for the learners and an uncompromising quest for excellence are all important.
>
> Pedagogical competence (savoir) encompasses professional knowledge and skills, communication with pupils and staff and sound pedagogical reasoning and decision making. All of these skills must be modelled as they lie at the heart of the practice of educating others
>
> Teaching skills (savoir-faire) are the tools required to transmit pedagogical competence. A teacher centred approach, incorporating effective communication, feedback and opportunities for reflection, is essential to effective role modelling.

But how do we learn from role models? We need to look for some or all of the foregoing qualities in those from whom we choose to learn. We also need to be selective. The most popular person may not be the best role model. We can be positive about approaching a role model and asking politely to team teach or reflect or to discuss plans and activities. Most people would be pleased to be viewed as a potential role model. You can pick who you emulate from colleagues by looking at the class and seeing how the children respond to the teacher. We, the authors, all seek out people with a kind demeanour, who are positive role models all of the time, not just in the classroom. We also avoid people who show off; quiet competency is better. We look for proven solidity in teaching, avoiding people who are 'against' the child. We also seek out opportunities for team teaching and for working together. Peer support is crucial to the wellbeing of teachers.

Speaking about learning from nursing, Morton-Cooper and Palmer (1993) cite Nelms et al. (1993), who help keep in sight what is important about learning from each other.

> The secret, we believe, is related to teaching caring encounters of an ethical kind, perhaps even a type of love, not of the romantic kind, but a learning entanglement in which

admiration for the knowledge and competence of a caring expert, curiosity about the subject matter of our discipline and feelings of amazement and excitement are evoked in the learner throughout the process of acquiring knowledge and skills.

(Nelms et al., 1993, p. 23)

Role modelling is an important way we learn to be who we are professionally, and role modelling is important for senior staff in the organisation to provide leadership in what is appropriate and desirable behaviour.

Role modelling vignettes

The following role modelling vignettes are intended as an approach to illuminating the process by which we can learn from others.

After school

A concerned beginning teacher phones her principal teacher, Mrs. Smith, at home to tell her that a pupil's behaviour had made her angry and aggressive and she doesn't know what next steps she should take to improve her relationship with the pupil. The principal teacher is obviously annoyed at being called 'out of school.' Although she responds to the teacher's anxieties and finally reassures her, the conversation is unpleasant and filled with tension, as Mrs. Smith is abrupt to the point of rudeness.

In the staffroom

In the staffroom, students and teachers overhear Mr. Patterson, a member of school management, describing a teacher in derogatory terms and using the teacher's name. One of the teachers asks to speak to Mr. Patterson privately and reminds him that he is in a public place, violating staff confidentiality and failing to show respect.

In the headteacher's office

A beginning teacher finds that a pupil with dyslexia is upset and worried about coping with the demands of the curriculum. The headteacher, Dr. Jones, is extremely busy, with many parents and other stakeholders waiting. Nevertheless, he invites the teacher and pupil into his office, sits down and takes the pupil's hand, empathises with the teacher's and the pupil's concerns and explains that he is very pressed for time; he also arranges a special appointment with both at a later date when he will have time to reassure them and answer their questions.

So, what might these vignettes tell us?

What might be the requirements of the role model?

First, one should be aware of *being* a role model. The conscious recognition of the importance of role modelling as a teaching and learning strategy, and the positive or negative impact of what we are modelling, is fundamental to improving performance. For example, is Mrs. Smith (vignette 1) aware of the impact of her rude behaviour or of the fact that she is condoning it? We are role models at all times, when we are teaching and when we are in social situations, for example. We must also share our awareness with our students.

For example, it is important for Dr. Jones (vignette 3) to explain the encounter with the pupil at a later date so that the teacher will reflect on and understand some of the lessons learnt.

Second, we need time to practise our profession. Despite the challenges of teaching demands, we must protect time in order to talk, reflect and share findings, all of which are needed to make the lessons learnt through role modelling apparent. For example, had Mrs. Smith (vignette 1) talked about her personal distress in the evening, she would have given an important and positive message to the teacher. The lack of conversation led to a missed opportunity for learning. Negative attitudes, such as those shown by Mrs. Smith (vignette 1) and Mr. Patterson (vignette 2), are as powerful as the positive ones demonstrated by the role model in vignette 2 and Dr. Jones in vignette 3. Consciously modelling competence and kindness, as Dr. Jones demonstrates, can be transformative. However, we need to ensure that the behaviours being modelled are made explicit.

Many situations include a mix of positive and negative role modelling. We believe that reflecting on and sharing these experiences provides valuable lessons. For example, the teacher in vignette 2 demonstrates positive modelling through self-regulation. Dr. Jones (vignette 3) demonstrates his concern for both the teacher and the pupil in the midst of a hectic round of external exigencies. However, without thinking about these events, individuals may not learn from what they have observed. Although important components of role modelling will always remain implicit, a conscious effort to articulate what we are modelling, and to make the implicit explicit, will benefit both those who are learning from the role model and the role model him- or herself.

In conclusion, we must also remember that being an effective role model is an ideal to be pursued. No one is a perfect role model at all times. Awareness of our physical and emotional frailties and humility in dealing with them will stand us in good stead. Our objective, surely, is to be as consistently good as we can be.

We have considered role modelling in some detail as we consider it to be important to self-awareness and the cultural context. These three dimensions of professional learning support and underpin reflective practice.

Mentoring

Peer support and mentoring concern engaging in dialogue with people who have a shared commitment to learning through experience and who will prompt examination and discussion of different perspectives in practice (Butcher & Robertson, 2003). Having a mentor is a very good opportunity for learning. Sometimes, we are given a mentor. We hope your mentor has a way of being that makes you feel comfortable: Someone who is empathetic, experienced and non-judgemental.

Morton-Cooper and Palmer (1993) describe the attributes, qualities and abilities of an effective mentor in a nursing context. We have adapted this for a teaching context.

- Has appropriate knowledge and experience and able to command respect;
- Has ability to build on mentee's strengths and offer constructive feedback;
- Is a reliable source of information;
- Is able to promote good judgements.

The mentor has confidence to:

- Be imaginative;
- Demonstrate initiative, take risks and have personal power that is used appropriately;
- Seek new challenges and initiatives;
- Lead and offer clear direction;
- Share credit for achievements;
- Be able to deal with another's problems, challenges and triumphs.

The mentor is committed to:

- Continuing professional development;
- Having a keen interest in seeing others develop and advance;
- Investing time, energy and effort into the working relationship;
- Personal motivation and a desire to motivate others.

(Morton-Cooper & Palmer, 1993, pp. 73-74)

Interestingly, Morton-Cooper and Palmer (1993) describe toxic mentoring, which we have adapted here.

- The mentor uses the mentee and takes any credit due;
- Uses the mentee's abilities to further his or her own career;
- The power in the relationship remains with the mentor, resulting in manipulation, over-protection, dependency and lack of development;
- Control and excessive direction, causing the mentee to conform and resulting in cloning.

There is inevitably a power dynamic at play with mentoring with the mentee being lower in the social hierarchy than the mentor. Karen gets around this by having a symbiotic mentoring relationship with a friend and colleague, taking it in turns to be mentor to each other, and this works well.

Staying well

Trying new things and growing and developing are fundamental to the career of the teacher. Ways of staying well with a busy workload involve seeking peer support and being able to share feelings and ideas. They also involve being there for other people in a reciprocal relationship. Reflection is important. We need in a busy job to be aware that we cannot do everything at once and all of the time. We all go home after a class that did not work well feeling low, but we can talk to others and reframe it positively as a learning situation and balance it against all the times when things have been good, if not wonderful.

Camaraderie keeps Penny going, and the joy of a smile and light-bulb moment for the child. Teachers need to know they do make a difference and, indeed, they do. Teachers are part of the formative times of the lives of children and make a difference for the child's whole life. Alison and Penny explain the privilege of being part of this life story, of making a difference.

When did I make a difference?

When I, Alison, became principal teacher of modern languages (ML), it was customary for 'able' pupils to continue with their studies in French and/or German until national exams were sat. These were ordinary 'O' grades at the end of S4 (age 15) and 'Highers' at the end of S5 (16-17). Those pupils for whom an ML was not considered to be appropriate, for whatever reason, were removed from MLs after S2 (age 12).

Traditionally, longer serving members of the department staff taught the upper stages, taking them through examination curricula. This was considered a 'perk' of the years spent teaching. The early stages were taught on a chronological basis; the newer the teacher, the younger the classes, the greater the challenge because of the size of the classes and the 'ability' range of the pupils and the greater the risk of bad behaviour and exclusions.

I enjoyed teaching the younger pupils, and if I'm truthful, there was an element of Jean Brodie-ishness* in my way of being with them: If I could enthuse them, motivate them, challenge them in security, laugh with them and inspire them, then they would be 'mine for ever!' Or at least, they would stay in an ML classroom for longer than two years!

The headteacher was keen to let me try things out as long as I was monitoring the process and the product. In the first instance, I would take the younger classes and my colleagues would focus on S3 (age 14) classes upwards. Lessons were built around themes, such as Le Village and Le Gratte-Ciel, and involved the children using the language they were learning in a realistic context.

They formed 'families' living in the village or the high rise; they created their house and their household; they chose the job they wanted to do; they went shopping and made meals; they went to cafés and restaurants; they showed tourists around their village; they had arguments about what they liked and what they didn't like and so on. For those of you who studied an ML at school, you can see how easy it was to take relatively simple ideas and to bring these alive in an organic, free-flowing and hugely enjoyable manner. It involved a lot of work between lessons as the children were deciding where all this language could take them, but oh it was grand! And how they learned!

When it came time for the pupils to make their subject choices at the end of S3, I was thrilled to see that the number who had opted to continue with their foreign language had risen to almost 75%! And this continued thereafter when choices were being made for higher examination classes.

I think I made a difference because the pedagogy was enabling, the contexts were fun and challenging, the children knew they had a voice in decision making and it felt right for all of us.

*This refers to the book *The Prime of Miss Jean Brodie* by Muriel Spark, in which the teacher is devoted to her pupils.

> **Penny making a difference**
>
> I often wonder how many teachers realise how much of a difference they make to their pupils on a daily basis, as well as long term. I've been very lucky to hear from a few different past pupils who have returned to school to see me, and I have been thrilled to hear how well they are doing: One girl finished university and is now, significantly, a hydraulic engineer; a boy is at university training to become a dentist, whilst another is training to become a doctor. In many schools this may be normal, but many of our children do not come from affluent backgrounds and are the first in their families to go to university. All of these pupils have said it was our discussions about their futures that helped them move forwards in their lives. I'm equally thrilled to hear from any past pupil, when they return to visit, asking 'Do you remember when … ?' which is often linked with a kind gesture always encouraged in class. I also once bumped into a past pupil (now an adult) who reminded me of her being sick on the way back from a school trip, which I cleared up. She said it always reminded her to be helpful and kind when someone needed you.

We need only re-read John's accounts of his work as headteacher, enthusing and inspiring colleagues, parents, carers and not least children in his school. His particular professional context reminds *all* teachers that whilst curriculum knowledge and curriculum coverage are important for the children we teach, what enables these is intimate knowledge of their capacities, their skills, their interests, their foibles, their source of fun and enjoyment and our willingness to work as part of a caring, valuing team.

Learning points

1. Our work in progress of becoming a good teacher never ends. Observation, noticing and listening are crucial to being a good teacher, and they are linked to knowing self.
2. Thinking of new initiatives, the key question to ask is "what is the pedagogical justification for this?" If it is a worthwhile initiative, it needs time to be embedded.
3. Reflexivity challenges taken-for-granted assumptions.
4. A culture or ethos of working positively together, learning from each other and supporting and celebrating good practice is vital.
5. We need time to practise our profession and protect time to talk, reflect and share.
6. And we need to stay well. We cannot do everything at once and all of the time.

Challenge questions

1. What is the nature of habitus for you? What history makes you who you are? How does this affect your practice?

2. Thinking about 'field,' what is your role as a player in the field of your school or university?
3. Can you think of an example where your self-awareness, or lack of it, led to learning?
4. Can you think of a situation where you used professional artistry and reflected in action?
5. Do you have role models or mentors who influence you in your practice? What qualities do they have that assist you to learn? What knowledge, skills or qualities do you have to assist others?
6. Thinking about yourself under pressure, what do you do or could you do to stay well?

References

Boud, D. (2010). Relocating reflection in the context of practice. In H. Bradbury, N. Frost, S. Kilminster, & M. Zukas (Eds.), *Beyond reflective practice: New approaches to professional lifelong learning*. Routledge, London.
Butcher, H., & Robertson, J. (2003). Individual and organisational development for community practice: an experiential learning approach. In S. Banks, H. Butcher, P. Henderson., J. Robertson (Eds.) *Managing Community Practice; Principles, Policies and Programmes*. Policy Press, Bristol, UK.
Collier, K. (2010). Re-imagining reflection: Creating a theatrical space for the imagination in productive reflection. In H. Bradbury, N. Frost, S. Kilminster, & M. Zukas (Eds.), *Beyond reflective practice: New approaches to professional lifelong learning*. Routledge, London.
Deer, C. (2021). Reflexivity. In M. Grenfell (Ed.), *Pierre Bourdieu: Key concepts*. Routledge, London, UK.
Dewey, J. (1986). September. Experience and education. In *The educational forum* (Vol. 50, No. 3, pp. 241-252). Taylor & Francis Group.
Fook, J. (2010). Beyond reflective practice: Reworking the 'critical' in critical reflection. In H. Bradbury, N. Frost, S. Kilminster, & M. Zukas (Eds.), *Beyond reflective practice: New approaches to professional lifelong learning*. Routledge, London.
Fook, J., & Gardner, F., (2007). *Practising critical reflection: A resource handbook*. McGraw-Hill Education (UK), Maidenhead, Berkshire, UK.
Frost, D. (2010). Professionalism and social change: The implications of social change for the reflective practitioner. In H. Bradbury, N. Frost, S. Kilminster, & M. Zukas (Eds.), *Beyond reflective practice: New approaches to professional lifelong learning*. Routledge, London.
Fuller, S. (2012). Conatus. In M. Grenfell (Ed.), *Pierre Bourdieu: Key concepts*. Routledge, London, UK.
Holstein, J., & Gubrium, J. (2000). *The self we live by: Narrative identity in a postmodern world*. Oxford University Press, New York, NY.
Hoyrup, S., & Elkjaer, B. (2016). Reflection: Taking it beyond the individual. In D. Boud, P. Cressey, & P. Docherty (Eds.), *Productive reflection at work*. Routledge, London.
Maton, K. (2012). Habitus. In M. Grenfell (Ed.), *Pierre Bourdieu: Key concepts* (2nd dE.).. Routledge, Abingdon, Oxon, UK.
McArdle, K., & Hurrell, A. (2016). The man in the rubber suit: A strong core of qualities and the contribution to professional development. In T. Norton (Ed.), *Professional development: Recent advances and future directions*. Nova Publishers, New York, NY.
Mezirow, J. & Associates. (2000). *Learning as transformation: Critical perspectives on a theory in progress*. Wiley Jossey-Bass, San Francisco, CA.
Morton-Cooper, A., & Palmer, A. (1993). *Mentoring and preceptorship: A guide to support roles in clinical practice*. Blackwell Science, Oxford, UK.
Nelms, T., Jones, J., & Gray, D. (1993). Role modelling: A method for teaching caring in nursing education. *Journal of Nursing Education*. 32, 1, pp. 18-20.
Palmer, P. J. (2017). *The courage to teach* (20th Anniversary Ed.). Wiley, Jossey-Bass, San Francisco, CA.
Polanyi, M. (1962). Tacit knowing: Its bearing on some problems of philosophy. *Reviews of Modern Physics* 34(4), p. 601.
Schön, D. (1987). *Educating the reflective practitioner*. Jossey-Bass, San Francisco, CA.
Smith, C. (2010). *What is a Person?* University of Chicago Press, London.
Thomson, T. (2012). Field. In M. Grenfell (Ed.), *Pierre Bourdieu: Key concepts* (2nd ed.). Routledge, Abingdon, Oxon, UK.
Vanier, J. (1998). *Becoming human*. House of Anansi Press, Don Mills, Ontario, Canada.

17 Conclusion

Conclusion

The consensus of the authors is that the role of the teacher has become more and more difficult to implement over the years. Performativity has taken hold of schooling. Constructs around accountability and performance to externally defined agendas have put pressure on teachers. There has been what Priestley and Minty (2013) refer to as 'two decades of intrusive input and output regulation' (p. 125). Inputs and outputs are reminiscent of the old-fashioned manufacturing, factory way of working. Conversely in Scotland, there is perceived to be increased anxiety over the enhanced teacher autonomy provided by the Curriculum for Excellence of the Scottish Government (Priestley & Minty, 2013).

Mead (2020) describes how teaching is a largely emotional way to work, and performativity has an effect on the teacher who cannot bring a personal mission to the classroom, because the mission is frustrated by micro-management and regulated regimes. Teachers who distinguish themselves from this and simply perform will perform with cynicism. Teachers who try to change the systems may suffer burnout and those who seek to teach within the system, we suggest, and within personal morality will feel frustrated.

The worth of education is affected not just by the quality of the individual teacher, although we think this is of primary importance. It is also determined by the environment and systems within which teachers work. Measurements of effectiveness of education rarely focus on this dimension of the individual teacher's performance. Drawing again on Priestley et al.'s (2017) research, contextual conditions of schooling are not analysed and questioned in the same way and to the same extent as teacher quality, which is often, we suggest, seen through the lens of student achievement. Student achievement still begs the question of what is education for? It is, we argue, for those things that are immeasurable in tests, as well as measurable skills and outcomes.

We suggest that the individual teacher is the most important feature of an education system, but the system itself is in need of means and methods of systemic change. Learning outcomes and competences or capabilities, which seek to itemise what is done in the classroom, attract criticism about whether it is ethical to predefine what children should learn and who they should be; how outcomes are framed and the (lack of) links to other areas of the curriculum; and how teachers individually make sense of learning outcomes (derived from Priestley et al., 2017).

Does the teacher have time to give the children time?

In the following conversation with Lynne, a colleague and critical friend, Alison discusses the idea that the curriculum limits teachers' time to give children the time. The teachers need time to learn too.

Alison: Do you think perhaps it's the formal curriculum that's imposing strictures on the teacher's use of time, to give the children time to learn?

Lynne: I think it's definitely the curriculum that's imposed every change that's happened, as opposed to change that emanates from what's going on in the classroom. And very often it's top-down: the teachers are not developing that curriculum. That's being imposed, therefore they don't have agency, they don't have that deeper, worked-through understanding. They've not been given the time and space to come to terms with the next thing that's being required of them.

And I can remember that with 5-14 (a new Scottish curriculum) coming in, I decided in our department that we would be working on English language and collectively we would develop that ... and that was fine. That was how we were doing it.

And then in came the instruction from the region (managers of the curriculum), that we had to be introducing environmental studies (ES), which was in the latest document to be issued. My plan was that we would just take our time looking through each of the documents because the children were still getting ES in science and all sorts.

And so, in order to oblige or to conform to what we were being asked, I went through and made up an applied teaching plan for the ES document because I knew it was too much for the teachers. But it didn't help them. That really didn't help them. So possibly, it's not just for children. We all need time and space to learn.

Surely

We shall conclude this book with another piece from Alison, with Ellie and Paul, parents of Lily. Lily is now 12 years old and has moved on to secondary school. Ellie and Paul are pulling their thoughts together as the conversation comes to an end.

Alison: So how do you think we could try to get this right?

P: Well, understanding individuals, which I know is a huge task. There are some teachers who choose the way of control, an imbalance of power between them and the children ... shouting, so quick to judge ... and then, there are others who use their own love and enjoyment of a subject to help that rub off on the people in their class. In the busy life of the classroom and the busy life of the teacher, that doesn't take more time. They have so little of it anyway. It just takes a little bit of effort and a bit of exuberance and passion for your profession. Teaching is about inspiring and encouraging and helping our children flourish and grow under our tutelage or whatever it be.

E: I was talking to a wee boy just before the summer holidays and asked him who his teacher was going to be in primary 7 (age 11-12). And he said, I hope she 'gets' me. I hope she smiles; I hope she makes me happy.

P: Do teachers know how to engage their pupils, how to have them on the edge of their seats, waiting for the next new thing to be shared? Teaching our children is such a wonderful opportunity and a privilege to help mould these young people into young adults and to be wonderful, happy members of society. We hear lots of negative things about teachers and teaching, but when there's energy and vibrancy, surely it can be such a wonderful experience for the children.

Alison: Now Lily's story is only one story, only one fairly extreme story of what didn't go right for one child. Her experiences are recounted here by her parents, through one optic you might say. But if we multiply that one child by the number of classes, by the number of schools in the UK, it's really frightening and demoralising.

But surely, we can try to be the kind of teacher Ellie and Paul want for children – passionate, inspiring, encouraging, nurturing … surely?

Finally, values again

The subtitle of this book is *Values in Educational Practice*, as this is what we consider to be important for the good teacher. The beliefs and values of teachers are so important. There is a widespread view in academic literature that teacher beliefs are formed early in a teacher's career. Indeed, others suggest that the majority of beliefs are formed through early life experiences, such as their own schooling (Priestley et al., 2017). We do not believe that beliefs are fixed, and we believe they can change over time and be flexible. Fundamental to teachers' beliefs is their understanding of the purpose of education. We discussed this briefly in Chapter 2, and this understanding is implicit in all the other chapters. Priestley et al. (2017) undertook research with teachers and found that many teachers viewed the purpose of education in rather instrumental terms, seeing it as a set of particular aims our outcomes, rather than focusing on the bigger question of what education is actually *for*.

These aims seemed to be about predetermined capacities and dispositions, which were more about equipping pupils to 'fit in' rather than providing the skills to handle uncertainty and to be agents of change. Furthermore, Priestley et al. (2017) found that teacher aspirations in respect of their teaching were relatively short term in nature and the day-to day planning was done with short-term goals in mind. They suggest that much teacher action is shaped by short-term aspirations to tick curricular boxes, deliver enjoyable lessons, keep pupils engaged and interested and keep classes quiet and well behaved. These aspirations are not to be put aside, we suggest; the key is to do this but hold onto the purpose of education and what it is for.

Accordingly, teachers need to be looked after; in our view, they need:

- In teacher education, an opportunity to explore who they are, their values and beliefs, along with the link to how and what they teach;
- A level of autonomy that allows for creativity in the classroom;
- Time, place and spaces that are conducive to learning;
- Performance measures that are complex enough and sophisticated enough to recognise and take account of the context in which the teacher is working;
- As above, and measures that are developmental, not purely judgemental;

- Reward for creativity and imagination used to promote critical thinking and problem solving in the classroom;
- Support systems from seniors and colleagues that promote creativity and resilience;
- Appropriate recompense for the sophistication and responsibility of the work.

With these provided, perhaps Ellie and Paul and Lily would have had a better experience of education.

The last word goes to Penny, who casts a note of caution, based on her experience. There is no such thing as the perfect teacher.

> Students don't need
> a perfect teacher.
> They need a teacher who is trying;
> A teacher who will laugh at their own typos
> and apologize for the bigger mistakes.
> A teacher who is not afraid to look silly
> or say that they don't know the answer.
> A teacher with high expectations and who,
> every day, gives each student a blank slate
> and a genuine smile.

References

Mead, N. (2020). *Values and professional knowledge in teacher education.* Routledge, Abingdon, Oxfordshire, UK.

Priestley, M., Biesta, G., & Robinson, S. (2017). *Teacher agency: An ecological approach.* Bloomsbury Publishing, London.

Priestley, M., & Minty, S. (2013). Curriculum for Excellence: 'A brilliant idea, but ... ' *Scottish Educational Review* 45, 39–52.

Index

Page numbers in *italic* indicate figures.
Page numbers by n indicate notes.

Aboriginal people (Australia), learning and traditional life 23
actor network theory (ANT) 73-74, 77
Additional Support Needs (ASNs) 19, 38, 121; and modern languages classes 54-55
Adoniou, M. 109-111
Amabile, T.M. 95
Anderson, E.S. 125
anecdotes on school and past teachers (authors) 13-14, 21, 24
Applying nurture as a whole school approach (ANWSA) 92-93
artistic skills, as required by teachers 86
Aslanian, T.K., and Moxnes, A.R. 75-76
attachment theory (emotional child development): nurture groups 90; place and belonging 75
attention deficit hyperactivity disorder (ADHD), and nurturing 89, 92
attunement 61-62
Australian Curriculum for subject English (ACARA, 2012) 110-111
autonomous learners 94
autonomy 75

bad language 35
Ball, S.J. 42-43
Ballatt, J., and Campling, P. 22
Bandura, A. 121
Barr, M., and Tschannen-Moran, M. 101
Beck, D., and Purcell, R. 128

behaviour management system: nurturing school 94; school discipline 66
beliefs (development Dworkin) 16-17
Belonging: A culture of place by bell hooks (Cooper) 74
Ben-Peretz, M. 108
Bennathan, M., and Boxall, M. 90
Better Behaviour through Golden Time (Mosley) 47
Biesta, G. 80, 120
Black, P., and Wiliam, D. 76
Blömeke, S., et al. 106-107
Bolton, G. 10, 26
Boud, D. 138
Bourdieu, P. 134
Boxall, M. 92-93; and Bennathan, M. 90
breakfast provision (school) 6, 23, 45, 125
Brighouse, T. 102
Bronfenbrenner, U. 3-4
Bruney, G. 34, 112
Burns, J., et al. 94
business discourse 17-18

Caine, V., and Clandinin, D.J. 24
Camic, P.M., and Clift, S. 86
Campling, P., and Ballatt, J. 22
caring, relational and reciprocal view 88
Caring (Noddings) 88
Carr, D. 15
Center for Courage & Renewal 39
circle time 92

Clandinin, D.J., and Caine, V. 24
Clarke, T. 99; Löhre, A. and Platt, R. 80; and Platt, R. 80, 83-84
classroom management: 'behaviour management' 66; books and guidance 47; children with demanding behaviours 67; cohesion and learning outcomes 69; internal obstacles (ignoring) 67; James (Alison's case study) 67; and kindness 46-47; no place for bullying (Hattie) 69; Penny's story 68; physical changes to classroom 94; social reinforcement 66; strategies (Palardy) 66; struggling to 'control' 46-47; tolerance and patience 65-69
Clegg, S., and Rowland, S. 42
Clift, S., and Camic, P.M. 86
clothing swaps 6
cognitive development, music training/experiences 86
collaboration: pitfalls 101-102; successful and meaningful 101
Collard, P., Looney, J. 95
collective efficacy 101, 121
collective self-perception 101
community of practice 22
Connelly, M., et al. 112
continuing professional development (CPD) 38, 67, 103
Cooper, J.A. 74
cost of living crisis, affects 6
courage 50-57; Additional Support Needs (ASNs) 54-56; appropriate courageous behaviour 51; challenge questions 56; for the child 51-52; curriculum and creativity 55-56; definition 50; learning points 56; McWhinnie case study (use of Homer's *Odyssey*) 55-56; modern languages classes (ASNs) 54-55; in the organisation 52-54; outdoor learning (case study) 52-54; overcoming fear (Mandela quote) 50; principles of inclusion 55; psychological 52; social 52; social justice 128-129; teaching algebra 51
Courage to Teach (Palmer) 50
Coutts, N., and McArdle, K. 113-114
Covid-19 pandemic: lockdowns 4, 37; safeguarding 37
creative tension, espoused values and actual practice 10
creativity and the arts: arts definition 86; nurturing creativity 95; wellbeing 85-86

Cresswell, T. 74
critical reflection 137-139; being critical definition 10; ethics and values 9-10; purpose 138; social justice 127-128
critical reflectivity 26
critical thinking (encourage) 84
Crowley, S. 47
cultural sensitivity, rural schools 7
cultural values, beliefs and practices 4
curriculum: and 'teaching' 26; time limits 148; time to cover 76; wellbeing and attainment-driven 80

Davies, J. 39-40
de Souza, R. 4
Dean, C. 28
Deer, C. 134
Department for Education Teaching Standards 98
Derewianka, B. 110
Dewey, J. 22, 76
Dix, P. 47, 68-69
Donohoo, J. 101, 121
Dor-Haim, P., and Nir, A. 52
Dorling, D. 9, 126-127
Doyle, R. 94
Dusting Off the Thunderbolts (Jones) 100
Dworkin, G. 16-17

ecological systems theory (Bronfenbrenner) 3-4
education: composite purposes (Biesta) 80; constituents 25; for democracy 117-118; economic targets 80; information-driven pedagogy 113, 117; learning as transformation 137; purposes 17-18, 25, 80, 118-120, 147, 149; socially constructed 15; structural functionalist view 10-11; understanding and problem solving 24; and wellbeing 79-80
education changes (authors would make) 18-19
education (defining) 25-26; in gardening terms 25, 88
Education Empowerment Fund pilot project 101
educational discourses: and business discourse 17-18; and discourses of kindness 43-44; neo-liberal discourse (influence) 63, 125
Edwards, R., and Fenwick, T. 73
Eells, R. 121
Elkjaer, B., and Hoyrup, S. 138
Ellis, J. 75

empowerment: challenge questions 64; everyday routines 62-63
England: Ofqual regulatory framework 125; teachers' professional standards 98
English as an additional language (EAL) 5
Estola, E., et al. 21-22
ethics: critical reflection 9-10; good and evil concepts 18
expertise, needs and challenges 15
extracurricular activities (free) 19

Fenwick, T., and Edwards, R. 73
Ferguson, Z. 44-45
Filipović, K., and Hayes, N. 88
flourishing 17, 118
Fook, J. 138-139; and Gardner, F. 26, 138
forest school 53
Foucault, M. 24, 127-128
free extracurricular activities 19
free school meals 19; *see also* breakfast provision (school)
free swimming lessons (promoting safety) 125
freedom, positive and negative 18
French language learning, immersive experience (Alison) 60
Frost, D. 138
Fuller, S. 134
funding support (extra): authors' wishes 19; needs and challenges 38

games of values clarification 26
Gardner, F., and Fook, J. 26, 138
Gardner, H., and Gardner, G. 86
General Teaching Council, Scotland (GTCS): kindness 46; leadership definition 97; social justice, trust and respect, and integrity 7-8
Get the Buggers to Behave (Crowley) 47
Getting It Right for Every Child (GIRFEC) 19, 20n1, 46; indicators of wellbeing 80; SHANARRI 80, 94; wellbeing wheel *81*
global migration, language skills 5
Goffman, E. 113
'good' teacher early model 113-114
grammar teaching 135
Gramsci, A. 127-128
Gray, E., and Robinson, V. 102
Grimmer, T. 61-63
Grotberg, E. 38-39

groupthink 101
Gubrium, J.F., and Holstein, J.A. 24, 136

Haertel, H., and Walberg, H. 69
Hallam, S., and Ireson, J. 94
Harris, A. 97; Hopkins, D. and Leithwood, K. 98-103
Harrison, M., et al. 63
Harvey, D. 126
Hattie, J. 34, 38, 69, 97
Hayes, N., and Filipović, K. 88
health, definition by WHO 85
healthcare professionals, humility 60-61, 63
Higgins, C. 22
Holstein, J.A., and Gubrium, J.F. 24, 136
homework (compulsory/voluntary) 122
Hopkins, D., Harris, A. and Leithwood, K. 98-103
Hoyrup, S., and Elkjaer, B. 138
humility 58-64; and altruism 58-59; attunement 61-62; challenge questions 64; different cultures 63; healthcare professionals 60-61, 63; learning points 63-64; needs 60-61, *61*; power and empowerment 62-63; pupils struggling to understand 59-60; students' academic performance 59; teachers in Hong Kong study (Harrison) 63; unsung heroes 58; what humility bring to the classroom 58-59
Hurrell, A., and McArdle, K. 140

identity 134-137; desire for 95; formation 136; self and construct 136; stories of who we are 24
Ingersoll, R. 38
Injustice: Why Social Inequality Still Exists (Dorling) 126
Ireson, J., and Hallam, S. 94

Jones, J. 100, 103

kindness 42-49; breakfast provision anecdote (Karen) 45; challenge questions 48; and classroom management 46-47; community context 44; confusion with leniency 45; cultures of 44-45; dignity for pupils 47; displaced value 43; kind teacher (what makes) 47-48, *48*; learning points 48; learnt through experience 48; mark of good teacher 42; mind frames 45; performativity 42-43, 45; and professional values 46; and risk management

systems/structures 45; *savoir-être* (knowing how to be) 43-44, 140; softer old-fashioned virtues (Alison) 43-44; why it matters 44-46
knowledge 106-114; Australian Curriculum for subject English (ACARA, 2012) 110-111; challenge questions 114; circle of positive reinforcement 108-109; complex needs school 112; of content for teaching 108-111; 'good' teacher early model 113-114; hierarchies of knowledge 107-108; knowledgeable teacher 112; language functions 110-111; learning points 114; literacy 109-110, 118; mathematics education 106, 109, 111-112; pedagogical content knowledge 109, 111-112; radical constructivism 106; research about knowing (Ben-Peretz) 108; self-awareness 113; situated cognition 106; six knowledge domains (Adoniou) 109-110; social constructivism 106; technology education 108-109

Langhout, R.D. 75
language functions, knowledge 110-111
leadership 97-104; challenge questions 103; definition by GTCS 97; England 98; leadership practice 97-98; learning points 103; Scotland 98, 102-103; teachers' professional standards across UK 98; too many initiatives 103; Wales 98, 102
leadership practices 98-103; act of being bothered (Dix) 100; areas of deprivation and better-than-expected exam results 102; building relationships and developing people 100; building relationships as unrealistic expectation 100; building vision and setting directions 99-100; developing the organization to support desired practices 100-102; distributed leadership 101; groupthink 101-102; improving the instructional programme 102-103; maintaining orderly and safe environments 102; pupil voice (importance) 102; 'Seven Strong Claims of Successful School Leadership' (Leithwood, Harris and Hopkins) 98-103
league tables 120
learning (open and closed) 95
Ledwith, M., and Springett, J. 126
Leithwood, K., Harris, A. and Hopkins, D. 98-103
lesson plans, teach to the class in front of us 68, 121

libraries, importance 124-125
literacy: as functional achievement 118; knowledge 109-110, 118; as a 'unfreedom' 118
Löhre, A., Clarke, T. and Platt, R. 80
Looney, J., Collard, P. 95
Lucas, S. 94
lunchtime routines 94

Makaton signs/words, mathematics education 112
making a difference, authors 144-145
Maslow's hierarchy of needs 60, *61*
mathematics education: confusing language use 111-112; knowledge 109; Makaton signs/words 112; managing knowledge in practice 106; pedagogical content knowledge 109; self-awareness 135
Maton, K. 134
McArdle, K.: and Coutts, N. 113-114; and Hurrell, A. 140
McNicol, S., and Reilly, L. 90
Mead, N. 113, 147
Meighan, R., and Siraj-Blatchford, I. 10-11
mentoring: peer support 142-143; toxic 143
Mezirow, J., et al. 137
mind frames, kindness 45
Minty, S., and Priestley, M. 147
modern languages: and Additional Support Needs (ASNs) 54-55; French language learning (immersive, Alison) 60; making a difference 144
morality: common-sense view 16; values and teaching practice 16-17
Morris, J. 90-91
Morton-Cooper, A., and Palmer, A. 140-143
Mosley, J. 47
Moxnes, A.R., and Aslanian, T.K. 75-76
multicultural parents/family: fasting and prayer (Muslim faith) 36, 65, 122; language barriers 36; religious celebrations 36, 65; respect 36-37
music training 86
musical experiences 86

natural space 85; forest school 53
needs 60-61; identified 60; spiritual/higher order 60
Nelms, T., et al. 140-141
neo-liberal discourse (influence) 63, 125

neo-liberalism 125-127; competition and exploitation 126; erosion of workers' rights 126; right-wing populist politics 126; and UN Convention on the Rights of the Child (UNCRC) 127
'new professional' (Palmer) 56
Ng, A. 59
Nir, A., and Dor-Haim, P. 52
Noddings, N. 88-89
Nolan, A.D., et al. 94
Northern Ireland, teachers' professional standards 98
nurture groups 90-93; attachment theory (emotional child development) 90; closing the attainment gap 92; and equality gap 92; feature of home and school 91; how children learn from (Morris) 90-91; Kris case study 91-92; overcoming barriers to learning and attainment 90; play in 91-93; principles applied to whole-school 92; stigma 91-92
nurturing 88-96; and ADHD 89, 92; *Applying nurture as a whole school approach (ANWSA)* 92-93; or caring 88-89; challenge questions 95-96; creativity 95; guiding principles (McNicol and Reilly) 90; internet research 88-89; learning (open and closed) 95; learning points 95; pastoral roles of staff 94; transition to high school 89; whole-school approach 93-94
Nussbaum, M.C. 84, 116-117

Odegard, N. 76
Odyssey (Homer), gamification as Dungeons and Dragons style adventures 55-56
O'Sullivan, K. 47
outdoor learning (case study) 52-54

Palardy, J.M. 66
Palmer, A., and Morton-Cooper, A. 140-143
Palmer, P.J. 50, 56
panic attacks, wellbeing (Lily case study) 81-83
past pupils, doing well (made a difference to them) 145
pastoral roles of staff, nurturing 94
pedagogy: actor network theory (ANT) 74; information-driven 113, 117

peer support: mentoring 142-143; role modelling 140-141
performativity, terrors of 42-43, 45
'personal practical knowledge 112
Peters, R.S. 25
place and belonging 74-75; attachment theory (emotional child development) 75; challenge questions 77-78; home as exemplary kind of space 74; learning points 77; security and freedom 75; self-esteem 74; social construction of place 74-75
Platt, R.: and Clarke, T. 80, 83-84; Clarke, T. and Löhre, A. 80
play: created social worlds (children) 91; nurture groups 91-93; strengthening relationships 91
playtime routines 94
political decisions, new initiatives/short-term policies 5-6
Poor (O'Sullivan) 47
Poulson, L., and Wallace, M. 10
power relations, social justice 127-128
PPA time (planning, preparation and assessment time) 122
practice (moving forward) 133-146; challenge questions 145-146; conclusions 147-150; critical reflection 137-139; habitus and field 134; identity and self-awareness 134-137; learning points 145; making a difference 144-145; mentoring 142-143; 'professional artistry' (Schön) 139; reflexivity 139; role modelling 140-142; unspoken rules 134; wellbeing (teachers) 143-145
Priestley, M.: et al. 147, 149; and Minty, S. 147
Pring, T.: flourishing 17; moral virtues and intellectual virtues (distinction) 16; teaching as moral enterprise 25-26
'professional artistry' (Schön) 139
psychological courage 52
pupils: home learning activity/interest in school success 36; home life difficulties 35; home reinforcement of school decisions 36; kindness and dignity 47; structural functionalist view 11
Purcell, R., and Beck, D. 128

quality indicators, as quality of education itself 120

Rachels, J. 16
Rawls, J. 9
reading ability assessment 76-77
reflective practice 26-28; disturbance and uncertainty (stimulus) 138; examples (Karen and Clare) 27; reflection definition 137; self-reflexivity 136; teacher agency and social change 139; *see also* critical reflection
reflexivity 134, 139; social context 10-11
Reilly, L., and McNicol, S. 90
relational trust 39; as empathy 50
religious populations, needs 60
research interviews 15-16; classroom size and noise overwhelming 73; curriculum and time limits 148; good teacher requirements 5, 15-16, 46, 48; outdoor learning (case study) 52-54; reading ability assessment 76-77; self-awareness (trainee teacher Romans lesson example) 135; teachers' reflection time 76-77; 'theatres of learning' 75; transition to high school 89; wellbeing (Lily case study) 81-83, 118-119, 148-150
residentials 53
resilience (children's) 82; Grotberg model 38-39
resilience (teachers) 37-40; as bouncing back 14, 38; challenge questions 40; continuing professional development (CPD) 38; and Grotberg's children's model 38-39; pastoral care 38; Southeast Asian countries 14; support and coping strategies 39; teacher workforce trends in 1980s USA 38; Wester OECD countries 38
rights 116-123; challenge questions 123; education for democracy 117-118; entitlements 120-122; learning points 123; Lily (case study) 118-119; Muslim children 122; parents' rights 121-122; purpose of education 119-120; rights of the child in practice 118-119; teachers' (nothing found in literature search) 122; universal human rights 116-117
risk management systems/structures, and kindness 45
Robeyns, I. 117
Robinson, V. 99; and Gray, E. 102
Rohaan, E. 108-109
role modelling 140-142; difficult experiences (admission) 140; peer support 140-141; team teaching 140
role modelling vignettes 141-142

rote teaching 14, 24
Rowe, M.B. 76
Rowland, S. 42, 45; and Clegg, S. 42
rural schools: formal/informal curriculum 7; social influences 7; thematic approaches (composite classes) 6

safeguarding 36-37; Child Protection measures 37; Covid-19 pandemic 37; software system 36-37
Scheffler, I. 106
Schön, D. 139
school discipline, 'behaviour management' 66
school meals (free) 19; *see also* breakfast provision (school)
schools, invention of society 23-24
Scotland: areas of deprivation and better-than-expected exam results 102; Curriculum for Excellence 103, 147; teachers' professional standards 98
self-awareness 134-137; causal capacities 136; knowledge 113; nature or personhood 136; personal moral decisions 113; pupils' lack of interest 135; self-assessment 137; 'self-transcendence' 136
self-esteem, place and belonging 74
self-expression, desire for 95
self-regard, and humility 58
Sen, A. 117-118
'Seven Strong Claims of Successful School Leadership' (Leithwood, Harris and Hopkins) 98-103
Shafer-Landau, R. 9
Shulman, L.S. 106, 108-109, 111
Sieberer-Nagler, K. 67
Simmons, C. 84
Siraj-Blatchford, I., and Meighan, R. 10-11
Skillman, A.E. 74
smartphone ban 4
Smith, A. 125
Smith, C. 136
social context 3-11; challenge questions 11; for the child 3-4; critical reflection 9-10; influences affecting children's leaning 4-6; learning points 11; reflexivity 10-11; rural schools 6-7; values 7-9
social courage 52
social inequality: capabilities approach 9; persistence (reasons Dorling) 9, 126-127

social justice 124–129; action (what teachers can) 128–129; being equal and 'brute luck' 125; challenge questions 129; children from better-off families 125; critical reflection 127–128; General Teaching Council, Scotland (GTCS) 7–8; hegemony 127–128; injustice (five tenets, Dorling) 9, 126–127; interpretations 8–9; language sharpening (tell it as it is) 128–129; learning points 129; libraries 124–125; neo-liberalism 125–127; poverty 124; power relations 127–128; UN Convention on the Rights of the Child (UNCRC) 124–125
Socrates 117
special educational needs and disabilities (SEND) 38
special educational needs (SEN) 53
Spillane, J. 97
Spratt, J. 79–80, 84, 118
Springett, J., and Ledwith, M. 126
subject knowledge 51
swimming lessons (free, promoting safety) 125

teacher behaviour, authentic 34
teacher credibility 34
teachers: building relationships as unrealistic expectation 100; burnout/lack of work-life balance 122, 147; 'calling' 22; perfect (no such thing) 150; personal biography 22; personal moral decisions 147; PPA time (planning, preparation and assessment time) 122; role implementation (now more difficult) 147; time to give children time 148; wellbeing 143–145, 149–150
'teaching': activities and learning occurrences 25; and curriculum 26; moral enterprise (Pring) 25–26
teaching and learning responsibility (TLR) payments 98
team teaching 65; role modelling 140
technology education, knowledge 108–109
'theatres of learning' 75
Theorell, T., and Ullén, F. 86
Thompson, N. 62
Thomson, T. 134
time: coverage of curriculum 76; learning points 77; teachers' questions in class 76; teachers' reflection time 76–77; thinking time research (Moxnes and Aslanian) 75–76

tolerance and patience 65–69; challenge questions 69; classroom management 65–69; fasting and prayer (Muslim faith) 65; learning points 69; punitive behaviour management systems (Dix) 68–69; team teaching 65
transient year group 5
transition to high school, and nurturing 89
trust 33–41; attitude to learning 34; challenge questions 40; James (Alison's case study) 35–36; kindness to others 33; learning points 40; mistrust 34; with pupils 34–35; relational trust 39; respect multicultural parents/family 36–37
trust-based school culture, preconditions (Davies) 39–40
Tschannen-Moran, M., and Barr, M. 101
Tudge, J.R.H, et al. 4
Tyler, I. 125–127

Ullén, F., and Theorell, T. 86
UN Convention on the Rights of the Child (UNCRC) 46, 116–117; article (28) 116; article (29) 116; article (30) 116; and neo-liberalism 127; social justice 124–125
Universal Declaration of Human Rights (1948) 7, 118
universal human rights 7

'values' term 14
values schizophrenia 43
values (teaching practice) 13–20, 149–150; challenge questions 20; education changes (authors would make) 18–19; games of values clarification 26; judgements 14; learning points 19; moral virtues and intellectual virtues (distinction) 16; morality 16–17; purposes of education 17–18; social context 7–9
Van Manen, M. 15
vocation 21–28; altruism and degree of gratitude 22; authors' definitions 22–23; challenge questions 28; core teaching values 7; deep moral-ethical commitment 39; definitions 22–23; education (defining) 25–26; identity 24–25; implicit standards 23; learning points 28; reflection and reflexivity 26–28; teaching as 21–14; 'vocation' term 21–22
Vygotsky, L.S. 5–7, 106

Wadell, P. 60-61, 63
Walberg, H., and Haertel, H. 69
Wales: Curriculum for Wales Framework 102; teachers' professional standards 98
Wallace, M., and Poulson, L. 10
Walshaw, M. 109
Wealth of Nations (Smith) 125
wellbeing 79-86; attainment-driven curriculum alternative 80; challenge questions 86; children's experience (teachers, peers) 80; creativity and the arts 85-86; critiques 84-85; definition and dimensions 79; 'doing well' equating to academic attainment 80-81; factors that have impact 83-84; flourishing (Sen) 118; GIRFEC 80, 81; ideal school research (Simmons) 84-85; learning points 86; Lily (case study) 81-83, 118-119, 148-150; *loco parentis* 83; physical and emotional 118; purposes of education 79-80; research on feelings (Clarke and Platt) 80; teachers 143-145, 149-150; thinking and reflecting 80-83; WHO report 85
Wenger, E. 22
When Adults Change, Everything Changes (Dix) 47, 68-69
White, J. 17
Wiliam, D., and Black, P. 76
'world citizenship' 84
Worthington, E. 58-59

Young, M. 108

zone of proximal development (ZPD) 6-7

For Product Safety Concerns and Information please contact our EU representative GPSR@taylorandfrancis.com
Taylor & Francis Verlag GmbH, Kaufingerstraße 24, 80331 München, Germany

www.ingramcontent.com/pod-product-compliance
Lightning Source LLC
Chambersburg PA
CBHW082100230426
43670CB00017B/2909